The Electric Guitar

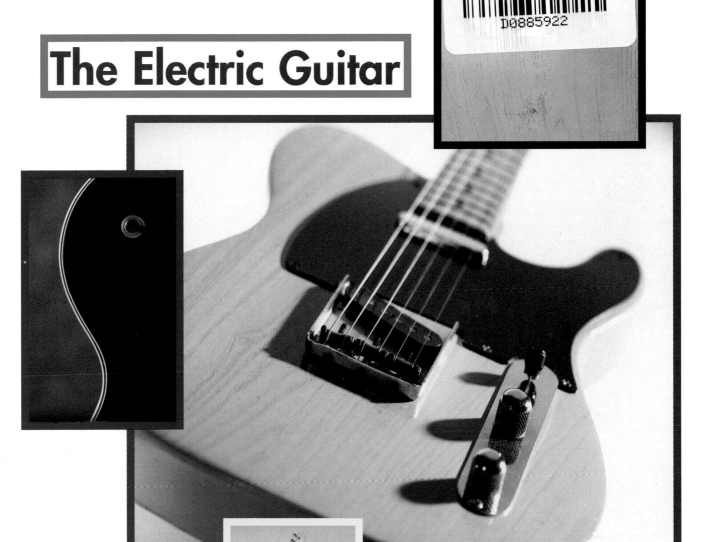

foreword by **Keith Richards**
edited by **Paul Trynka**
in conjunction with the **Design Museum**

the Electric Guitar

Contributors: Paul Trynka (All Guitar Profiles, Design Anatomy, Guitar Pioneers, The '50s)
Tom Wheeler (Visionaries)
Tony Bacon (Fender and Mass Production)
Douglas Noble (The '60s)
John Seabury & Charles Shaar Murray (In Search of Volume)
Dave Burrluck & Douglas Noble (The '70s, The '80s)
Dave Burrluck (The '90s)
Paul Day (The Rise of the Copy)

Book Design: Why Not Associates with Lucy Wise
Photography: Universal Fotografia (Profile shots: Steve Catlin, Jeff Kane)

First published in Great Britain in 1993 by Virgin Books, an imprint of Virgin Publishing Ltd.

This revised edition published in 2002 by
Virgin Books Ltd
Thames Wharf Studios
Rainville Road
London W6 9HA

Copyright ©: The Design Museum and Virgin Publishing Limited 1993; 2002

ISBN: 0 7535 0653 X

A catalogue record for this book is available from the British Library

Printed and bound by Graficas Reunidas (Spain)

All guitar profiles by Paul Trynka

Contents

by Keith Richards

Foreword

The electric guitar changed the way music was made. In essence it took over from the horn section of big bands – suddenly a trio or a quartet could achieve with an electric guitar what it would otherwise take a whole band to do. So in one way it put a lot of horn players out of work. In another way it made all of today's music possible.

The electric guitar is virtually a portable band, all by itself. All you need on top of that is a drummer. That one instrument revolutionized things and could make four or five guys into a band with an identity – it commercialized popular music, made it possible to play it more easily and spread it around much more quickly.

I've lost count of the guitars I've owned, but one thing I still think is amazing is the way that Leo Fender got so much right when he invented the Telecaster 40 years ago. And they still do the job now! So to me they're like a plumber's favourite wrench – I swear by them!

In its own way the electric guitar was vital in helping what I've achieved, or what the Stones have achieved. Where would I be without it?

Playing awfully quietly, for a start!

Left: T Bone Walker – the electric
guitar's first showman
Below: Eddie Lang, pictured here
with Bing Crosby, was a major
influence on the first generation of
electric guitarists

Guitar Pioneers

'Guitarmen, wake up and pluck – wire for sound, let 'em hear you play!' proclaimed the fast-rising guitarist Charlie Christian in 1939. His summons was to prove devastatingly effective. Christian saw the guitarist as a musician imprisoned in the rhythm section, condemned to plunk away like a robot in the big bands that had evolved over the previous decade; electricity provided a means of liberation.

But once unleashed, the electric guitar did not compete on equal terms with the saxophones and trombones Christian wanted to emulate – it rendered them obsolete. Invented in an era when the world was changing with the advent of mass communications and quantum mechanics, the electric guitar, in its turn, was to change popular music almost beyond recognition.

Today, the electric guitar is the most pervasive and influential of modern instruments, but at the beginning of the century the guitar was a comparatively minor instrument outside Europe, where a classical tradition had been established by the likes of Fernando Sor and Francisco Tarrega. Over the next decade, however, a strange alchemical reaction would take place. Perhaps the first witness to this was William Christopher Handy, who was waiting on a station platform in Tutwiler, Mississippi, one night in 1903. Stretched out on a hard bench he fell asleep, only to wake up some time later to the sound of a black musician in ragged clothes, fretting his guitar with a knife, and accompanying the mournful, vocal sound of his cheap guitar with a song about a local railroad line. W.C. Handy – who would later become known as 'the father of the blues' – was a schooled musician who understood the current styles of ragtime, gospel and classical music, but this was something entirely different. Somehow a tradition of African music had fused with Anglo/American folk song to produce an early form of the blues. In its turn this new tradition would go on to spawn jazz and rock'n'roll.

American music developed quickly over the next 20 years; in the South a combination of European influences resulted in hillbilly music, which became established with the advent of radio in the mid '20s and the consequent popularity of hillbilly acts such as Jimmy Rodgers and the Carter Family. At the same time a blues tradition was being established in Mississippi and Texas, by musicians like Charley Patton and Blind Lemon Jefferson. Over the same period the acoustic guitar started to become the dominant instrument for solo artists, thanks primarily to the Sears, Roebuck Company of Chicago. Sears were offering a range of seven acoustic guitars in their annual catalogue as early as 1894; by 1909 the range had increased to 12 guitars, the cheapest of which was priced at a mere two dollars.

Throughout the '20s, early blues and jazz musicians were already searching for new sounds, in a way exemplified by W.C. Handy's slide guitar player. Playing the instrument with a knife or bottleneck gave a fluid vocal feel that anticipated the electric guitar, but no one really knows where this technique originated. African musicians had used a one-string bow played with a slider, while Hawaiians had also experimented with different tunings. But although the Hawaiians were to influence blues slide playing, they hadn't originated it; the first known recording of Hawaiian guitar was made by Joseph Kekeku for Edison in 1909 – six years after Handy's encounter. By 1926, this technique had become relatively sophisticated, with musicians such as Blind Willie Johnson using the slide guitar to develop the expressiveness of a voice or saxophone.

Resonator Guitars At the same time that guitarists were experimenting with new playing techniques, they were also searching for more volume. Early experiments with resonator guitars aimed to increase the volume of an acoustic by coupling the strings to vibrating metal discs, or 'resonators' – the resulting guitars were eagerly purchased by early blues, jazz and Country musicians. The development of the valve amplifier by RCA in the '20s would prove a key event, and over the next few years guitarists would attempt to amplify their guitars with phonograph needles and microphones or telephone pickups. The young Lester Polfus – later to be known as Les Paul – was a typical, if pioneering, example.

'I started out doing Country bluegrass songs. I'd built my own radio and I heard this guy out of Chicago called Pieplant Pete. Now Pieplant is another name for Rhubarb, and that's how I got my first stagename – Rhubarb Red. So I copied what he did, sang like him, and it wasn't long before I got on the radio. Then a lot of gals were calling me and sending me cake, girls that knew Pete and thought he'd changed his name to Rhubarb Red. So I was getting his name, his cakes, and his girlfriends!

'Later on I began playing jazz, mainly because of Eddie Lang. I'd play Country music in the daytime to make a living, and then jazz at night, because I loved it.

'I'd started on the electric guitar in 1928, 'cause I thought I'd make more in tips if I could get heard properly. By the time 1931 came around I'd made up my mind not to play anything but the electric guitar so I needed an amplifier – I couldn't keep playing through my parents' radio! So I went to Belwin Hall in Chicago in 1931 and they made projectors to show movies on, and that's where I got my first proper amplifier.'

Eddie Lang – who played the conventional arch-top acoustics which were popular in jazz circles at the time – was probably the single biggest influence on what would be the first generation of electric guitarists. Possibly the most recorded guitarist of the '20s, he played with a range of musicians from Bessie Smith to Bix Beiderbecke. Lang also recorded a stunning series of guitar duets, under the black-sounding pseudonym Blind Willie Dunn, with blues player Lonnie Johnson, for the 'race' record company OKeh. Yet neither guitarist, as far as we know, pioneered electrics – Johnson would switch to electric after the Second World War, while Lang died in 1933 following a tonsillectomy operation.

The First Generation

By the time of Lang's death many guitarists of a practical bent, such as Les Paul, were experimenting with telephone pickups or phonograph needles – but none of them with results that attracted any attention. By 1932 the embryonic Rickenbacker company had persuaded several acquaintances to publicize their new lap-steel electrics – Jack Miller, a friend of Rickenbacker whizzkid George Beauchamp, had used his electric lap steel for performances at Hollywood's Grauman's Chinese Theatre as early as 1932. Yet although the lap steel – which is played on a guitarist's lap with the aid of a bottleneck or slider – was enjoying some popularity as musicians embraced Hawaiian styles, its exponents were not particularly influential, and were generally regarded as cranks or novelty acts.

Eddie Durham, however, was already building up a reputation as a guitarist with Bennie Moten's band when he decided he needed to make himself heard: 'With those big bands you couldn't hear the guitar – so I tried different ways to amplify the sound. I made a resonator with a tin pan – I'd carve out the inside of an acoustic guitar and put the resonator in there. When I hit the strings the pie pan would ring and shoot out the sound. Then I tried converting radio and phonograph amplifiers – with that rig I used to blow out the lights in a lot of places!'

Eddie Durham's guitar solo on The Jimmie Lunceford Big Band's 'Hitting The Bottle', recorded in September 1935, is generally cited as the first amplified guitar on record. Durham traded lines with vocalist Sy Oliver, bringing the guitar to the front of a big band for perhaps the first time. The instrument on this song was actually Durham's resonator guitar – Lunceford would grab the microphone and bring it up to Durham's guitar for the solos.

By 1936, Durham was using a guitar with an electric pickup for live dates, and becoming known as the instrument's principal exponent. He was one of a select few. Other pioneers included Floyd Smith, who played amplified Hawaiian guitar on Andy Kirk's 'Floyd's Blues', and Eldon Shamblin, guitarist with the pioneering western swing band, Bob Wills and his Texas Playboys. In 1937, Shamblin would become the first known Country musician to use a solid body electric guitar – the Rickenbacker Electro Spanish Model B. Played like a normal guitar, but with a tiny Bakelite body, the Rickenbacker only lasted for one engagement: 'Bob came over and said "Whatcha got?" I said "A guitar." He said, 'I don't want you to play it, because people won't know you're playin' a guitar. When I hire a guitar player I want him to look like a guitar player."' The hapless Shamblin returned to the unsatisfactory arrangement of amplifying his Gibson Super 400 with a phonograph pickup.

By 1937 several companies were producing lap steel and 'Spanish'-style electrics, but the instrument still attracted ridicule in 'serious' musicians' circles – Eddie Durham was still the only noted jazz player. But when Durham played with the Lunceford band in Oklahoma that year, he met a young guitarist who would become the instrument's first noted innovator, and win the electric guitar real credibility.

'We were there for about a month,' recalled Durham, 'and during the day we often jammed at a pool hall. One day Charlie Christian showed up with an old beat-up guitar that had cost him five dollars. He had big eyes to sound like a saxophone.'

Above: Floyd Smith, who played the first known electric Hawaiian guitar on record

Right: Eddie Durham was recording with an amplified guitar as early as 1935

'I made a resonator with a tin pan –
I'd carve out the inside of an acoustic
guitar and put the resonator
in there. When I hit the strings the
pie pan would ring and shoot out
the sound.'

Christian and Walker – the First Guitar Heroes

Charlie Christian had been working professionally since 1935, playing with his brother Edward in the Jolly Jugglers, but also working as a prizefighter, tap dancer and baseball pitcher. He had already built up a local reputation when he met Durham in 1937. Christian bought his first electric guitar, probably a Gibson ES150, soon afterwards, and by 1939 had been noticed by John Hammond, the talent spotter extraordinaire who also played a key part in the careers of performers such as Billie Holiday, Bob Dylan and Bruce Springsteen.

Hammond engineered an audition for Christian with Benny Goodman in California. Christian reportedly showed up for the audition in pointed shoes, a purple shirt and a string bow tie; the overworked Goodman was not initially impressed, but Hammond sneaked the young guitarist on to the bandstand for Goodman's performance that night at the Victor Hugo restaurant. Goodman counted in 'Rose Room', and there followed what Hammond described as 'the most explosive session I ever heard with Benny's crew'. Christian fed Goodman riff after riff, and sustained the song for over 45 minutes; the crowd went crazy, and Christian was hired on the spot.

During Christian's time with Benny Goodman he established the electric guitar as a solo instrument, with just as much expressive potential as the saxophone – the actual sound he made was unique, to the extent that on one celebrated occasion the young guitarist Mary Osborne mistook the sound of Christian's amplified guitar for that of a saxophone. Christian gave what was previously regarded as a gimmick real respectability; in a December 1939 *Downbeat* magazine he incited other guitarists to take up the electrified instrument:

'The dawn of a new era is at hand for all these fine guitarists who had become resigned to playing to feed their souls but not necessarily their stomachs. Electrical amplification has given guitarists a new lease of life.

'Amplifying my instrument has made it possible for me to get a wonderful break. A few weeks ago I was working for beans down in Oklahoma, having a plenty tough time of getting along and playing the way I wanted to play. So take heart, all you starving guitarists – I know that you play damned fine music, but now you've got a chance to bring the fact to the attention of not only short-sighted band-leaders, but to the attention of the world.'

Christian set out to prove that a guitarist was 'something more than just a robot plunking on a gadget to keep the rhythm going'. But his unconventionality went beyond the mere instrument he played; he explored dissonant notes, used hitherto unusual chords like the diminished seventh, and would deliberately deliver unsyncopated solos over syncopated backings – all techniques which anticipated the bop movement. Sadly, it was a movement in which he would not participate – after only two years with Goodman, he was taken ill with lung problems. Sent to Seaview Sanitarium on Staten Island, Christian was ordered to abandon his wild lifestyle, and was reportedly making excellent progress until a friend smuggled in a supply of marijuana and a woman. Charlie contracted pneumonia and died on 2 March 1941, at the age of 23.

Before Christian had enjoyed his two years of fame, he had formed a brief playing and dancing partnership with another musician who was keen on exploring the possibilities of the guitar: Aaron Thibeus Walker. Walker – T-Bone for short – was a blues player who was a fan of Blind Lemon Jefferson and Lonnie Johnson. Shortly after sharing gigs and guitar lessons with Christian, Walker moved to the west coast and acquired his first electric guitar – previously he'd played the banjo in order to achieve sufficient volume. Walker proceeded to blaze a trail for the electric guitar. After working with a string of bands through '30s L. A., he joined the Les Hite Orchestra in 1939, and cut the hugely influential 'T-Bone Blues' in June 1940. Through the '40s he would convert a whole host of nascent bluesmen to the electric guitar, including B.B. King, Lowell Fulson and Chuck Berry.

Walker's version of electric blues had many elements which would later become standard; the most fundamental of these, however, was the tone he used. The electric guitar had a sound which was fat and loud enough for single note playing, and would allow the guitarist to bend or add vibrato to single notes; all of these effects became part of T-Bone's armoury. Walker's recordings reveal an instinctive grasp of the electric's natural sound; the amplifier is turned up to the point where it aids the guitar's inherent sustain, and adds to the harmonic richness of the tone, making it as viable a solo instrument as the saxophone, but retaining its usefulness for rhythm work – the instrument's main staple up until then.

By the late '40s, when Walker had recorded his best-known hit 'Call It Stormy Monday', he was recording with a small, six-piece band. In this way he'd bridged the gap between the essentially solo Mississippi blues sound of Charley Patton or Robert Johnson, and the popular big band, making popular music accessible to small combos. Apart from its musical implications, this was a significant economic move which would later effectively spawn rock'n'roll, as well as the English R&B of bands like The Rolling Stones. The electric guitar was uniquely versatile, suitable for chordal rhythm work as well as for solo purposes. But although Walker was already offending jazz purists with his on-stage exhibitionism, playing the guitar behind his back, and engaging a scantily-clad dancer called (for obvious reasons) Lottie the Body, the instrument's outrageousness was still to be fully exploited. That would come with the advent of rock'n'roll.

Christian fed Goodman
riff after riff, and sustained
the song for over 45
minutes; **the crowd went crazy,
and Christian was hired
on the spot**

**Right and above: Charlie
Christian with Benny Goodman
(on clarinet). Apart from
pioneering the electric guitar,
Goodman's orchestra and sextet
were among the first racially
integrated outfits of the '30s**

Gibson ES150 | 1936

In 1935 the musical establishment considered the electric guitar to be the province of unmitigated weirdos – strange bakelite or aluminium instruments which were played by eccentric Hawaiian-shirted lap steel players or stetsoned hillbillies. The ES150, produced by America's most respected guitar company, and unofficially endorsed by some of the finest players of the era, would change all that. Although the ES150 was almost identical in construction to Gibson's existing L50 acoustic, the presence of an integral bar pickup close to the fingerboard meant this guitar was revolutionary.

Quite simply, the ES150 made the electric guitar respectable. As Gibson's first Spanish-style electric, it was the first notable electric guitar from a long-established company, and benefited from Gibson's marketing and distribution muscle. Other manufacturers might have beaten Gibson to it, but as far as most musicians of the '30s were concerned, the ES150 was the first electric guitar on the planet.

First commercially significant electric guitar

Designed 1934-1935

Commercially introduced 1936

Modified 1940 and 1946

Production life 1936-1956

Gibson were known to have experimented with electric guitars in the '20s; the company's maverick inventor Lloyd Loar had developed several electric designs, but failed to persuade Gibson to launch them commercially. By 1932 the Rickenbacker company was producing both solid lap steel electrics, and a conventional arch-top electric, the Electro Spanish; the appearance of these and other models doubtless persuaded Gibson president Guy Hart to resurrect the idea of producing an electric Gibson. Walter Fuller, who would later head the company's electronics workshop, joined Gibson the following year and was entrusted with the task of developing the necessary pickup.

Electric pickup technology was fairly primitive in the '30s; Rickenbacker's own pickup was of a 'horseshoe' design, whereby the magnets actually surrounded the strings. Fuller's design was more practical, using two solid nickel magnets below the strings; a one piece steel bar, surrounded by the pickup coil, directed the magnetic field towards the strings. By present day standards it was a bulky arrangement, but for the time it was serviceable, particularly as the two large magnets are situated below the guitar's top; only the blade polepiece, the bakelite coil cover with ivoroid binding, and the three mounting bolts are visible to the player.

Fuller's new pickup debuted on the company's first electric lap steel guitar, the EH150, which was in production by the beginning of 1936. The ES150 (ES standing for Electric Spanish) appeared slightly later. The general construction of the instrument was of conventional Gibson style, essentially identical to the L50 acoustic; it featured a 'Grand Auditorium' body, consisting of a solid spruce top with two f-holes, with a flat maple back and rims. The neck itself was made of solid mahogany, reinforced by the metal truss rod that Gibson had patented in 1922, and adopted the distinct 'V' profile typical of Gibson guitars of the period. The guitar featured Gibson's typical scale length of 24 3/4". The ES150's hardware was basic: a simple trapeze tailpiece and ebony bridge, adjustable for height by means of two thumb wheels. Electronics consisted of the aforementioned pickup, one

Gibson ES150 1936

'T-Bone had the first **electric guitar I ever saw, a Gibson.** I used to see him at the Rainbow Ballroom in Detroit around 1940, and he let me play it one time – I went out and bought one straight after. He was the father of the electric blues guitar.'

John Lee Hooker on T-Bone Walker

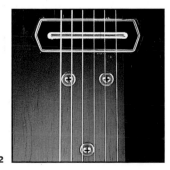

Main shot: 1939 Gibson ES150
1. This model features a carved maple back, as opposed to the flat back of the 1936 model
2. The 'Charlie Christian' pickup: the pickup's large magnets are hidden beneath the guitar's top

volume and one tone control, with the output jack located at the bottom of the tailpiece.

Although the Gibson company hailed their new $72.50 creation as 'a miracle' it took several years for the new instrument to take off. Few of the guitarists we now regard as electric pioneers, including Eddie Durham and T-Bone Walker, recorded seeing conventional electric guitars until approximately 1937. However, around that time both Walker and Charlie Christian purchased ES150s, and over the next four years would make the Gibson America's best-known electric; such was the extent of Christian's identification with the instrument that Walter Fuller's pickup became informally known as the 'Charlie Christian' pickup (Christian later also used Gibson's upmarket ES250, which featured the same pickup). By the time the guitar had achieved this fame Gibson had already modified the design, fitting a new type of pickup near the bridge in 1940. By 1946 the guitar had gained a new and slightly larger body, in which form it remained in production for another 10 years.

Although the ES150 was a groundbreaking insturment, the guitar itself is not now widely played; testing a 1939 example reveals why this is the case; although the actual acoustic sound is delightful, with a warm but slightly compressed tone, the amplified sound is sensitive to accidental knocks and bangs, while the electric sound muddies the notes within chords. Original ES150 users also found that the instrument's string response was somewhat unbalanced with the string gauges used at the time, the B string in particular being too prominent; Gibson subsequently attempted to minimize this by notching the blade polepiece around the B string. The neck's V profile is extremely comfortable, while a well-set up example allows for a remarkably comfortable action; although the guitar's electronics are basic by today's standards, the ES150 does demonstrate that even the company's budget models were extremely well-made.

Neither the Gibson ES150, nor the rarer Rickenbacker Electro Spanish which preceded it, fetch high prices in the collector's market. For all that, this first Electric Spanish model is among the most historic of any electric guitars, and despite its playing limitations there are many stunning recordings by Charlie Christian which demonstrate just how good it could sound in the right hands. Although many electric guitars are worth more money than this pioneering instrument, few are as significant.

Right : Adolph Rickenbacker, with 1932's Frying Pan
Below: Rickenbacker celebrate their 25th Anniversary, 1957

Visionaries:

The Inventors

Abomination! That was the word Segovia is said to have used in describing the very thought of an electric guitar. To take a serious concert–hall instrument whose history pulsed and sighed with legend, one associated with generations of small-shop European artisans whose craft was of the highest order, one whose romance was celebrated in poem and song, whose sublimely delicate tone depended on nature's own details like the grain pattern in the top – to take such a noble creation and plug it in, like some kitchen appliance, for God's sake, like a power tool, well, it was all too much for the Maestro.

But the intersection (collision, some would argue) of electricity and guitars was inevitable, for at least two reasons. First, there were plenty of people of the old school who sought to improve their beloved instrument's performance – to make it louder, for example, so that it could be heard amid the blaring horns and pounding drums of big bands; for them the shift towards amplification seemed as natural as the move from gut to wire strings. Second, there were people whose backgrounds were more closely associated with new technologies than Old World sensibilities, and for them the guitar was an irresistible guinea pig.

As much as we might like to discover one, there is no Abraham of the electric guitar's family tree, no single person whose incandescent genius and seminal work fostered all inventions that followed. At the base of the tree we find instead a tangle of roots. It's difficult to assess with precision the relative contributions of every participant, for various principal parties have incompatible recollections of key events, and there is even some disagreement over what constituted the first electric Spanish guitar. Was it an acoustic arch-top with a microphone stuck inside, or perhaps a lap steel with frets?

Despite the historical twists, it is undeniable that a few men of remarkable vision changed everything. Sometimes they collaborated. Sometimes they were arch rivals. Sometimes they worked in ignorance of each other. But together they brought forth an instrument that transformed most existing genres of popular music and would decades later energise a new hybrid dubbed rock'n'roll. For some, this electric guitar was nothing less than a new species, far removed from the heritage and aesthetics of its acoustic forebears. And yet several of its co-fathers were steeped in the most hallowed traditions of acoustic guitar. Lloyd Loar, for example.

The Lloyd Loar Legacy | Lloyd Loar came to Gibson's Kalamazoo, Michigan, plant in 1919, and over the course of his five-year tenure earned a reputation perhaps unparalleled in guitar history. Revered as virtually the Stradivarius of Kalamazoo, this engineer/ mandolinist/ composer/ lecturer/ inventor took over

of the Electric Guitar

Gibson's engineering and research departments, among others, and although he was not a builder himself he oversaw the creation of Gibson's breathtaking Master Model series, including the L-5, one of the most esteemed arch-top acoustics ever.

Despite a career of estimable renown in acoustic instrument circles, Loar proved to be something the staid folks in Kalamazoo never expected – a revolutionary. He designed an electric double bass in the '20s, a skinny, futuristic thing seemingly connected only by function to its enormous acoustic predecessors. (And according to researcher Richard Smith, by the late '20s, 'primitive, inefficient' electric guitars also existed.) Gibson didn't know what to make of it, and Loar left the company. He went on to found Vivi-Tone in 1933, and its guitars were distinctly un-Gibsonlike, with soundholes under the bridge, f-holes in the back, and pickups (the microphone-like elements that electrify guitars) mounted on a drawer that slid into the body from the side. He even built what could be called a solidbody, basically a full-length neck with a flat top attached to it.

Vivi-Tones were never produced in large quantities, and today even full-time collectors come across them only rarely. But with these guitars, Loar made a leap that would characterize design philosophies for decades to come. Instead of seeing electricity as a way to enhance a guitar's acoustic resonance, he sought to isolate its purely electric qualities so as to create something radically new. In a patent filed on 27 January 1934, he specified that his guitar could be used 'either as a generator, or a musical instrument, or *both*.'

Out of the Frying Pan ... | Some of Loar's contemporaries in faraway California were experimenting with similar concepts, and their instruments would prove to be landmarks in the electric guitar's adolescence. The late Adolph Rickenbacker, a Swiss tool and die maker and relative of air ace Eddie Rickenbacker, was a charter member of the Los Angeles guitar-building community of the '30s. The company that now bears his name claimed credit for inventing the electric guitar, with justification; its premier lap steel was the first electric manufactured on a commercial scale, and aside from Vivi-Tone, Rickenbacker (or its corporate predecessor, actually) was the first significant manufacturer of a solidbody electric Spanish model, in about 1935. (Spanish guitars are held upright in the conventional position, Hawaiian guitars flat on the lap.)

All accounts of Rickenbacker's entry into guitar manufacturing are tied to National founder John Dopyera and his brothers, with whom Rickenbacker had an enduring and bitter feud. In the eye of the hurricane was George Beauchamp (pronounced Beechum), a transplanted vaudevillian from Texas and early National partner. In 1969, Mr Rickenbacker recalled, 'George was the fellow who strapped one of those big phonograph horns on the body of the sounding board to make more music. He had the idea of mounting a radio speaker diaphragm inside the guitar.' Beauchamp was either a troublemaker who was allowed to associate with the Dopyeras only because of his financial connections (the Dopyeras' version), or he was an inspired inventor whose contributions allowed the Dopyeras to get off the ground and who was cruelly fired by them without regard for his family (Mr Rickenbacker's view).

In any case, George Beauchamp, along with Paul Barth, designed a small, skillet-shaped cast-aluminium lap steel guitar nicknamed the 'Frying Pan'. In the April 1974 *Guitar Player* magazine, historian Robb Lawrence quoted Barth's recollections that the two men worked on Beauchamp's kitchen table and in Paul's father's garage, labouring long hours and winding pickup coils on a sewing machine. After the last of many fallings-out, Beauchamp left National and the Dopyera brothers in about 1929 and joined Mr Rickenbacker. The result of that alliance would later be named The Electro String Instrument Corporation, manufacturer of Frying Pans – beginning in August 1932 – and other instruments.

National had been founded in Los Angeles by John Dopyera and his associates in early 1928, a couple of years after John and his brothers first registered the National trademark. After various business disputes became intolerable, Dopyera left in January 1929 to establish the offshoot Dobro Corporation, Limited. Both National and Dobro built 'resophonic', or 'ampliphonic', guitars, distinguished by their hubcap-like metal resonators (most Nationals had metal bodies; most Dobros had wooden bodies). Victor Smith went to work for Dobro at its inception and soon

designed and built an electric guitar, which Dobro manufactured and distributed. He swears that it predated Rickenbacker's Frying Pan.

'I began to work on electronics in my spare time,' he told me in 1977. 'When I joined the company, Dobro was making only resonator guitars – no electrics – but people wanted a louder sound, and everybody knew that electrics were the thing of the future. Trouble was, nobody knew how to build one. There were electrics before mine, but they didn't work. Most were based on using (pickup) units from telephones, phonographs, or microphones – the idea that a polepiece would break the magnetic flux, just like in a telephone. But I thought, you didn't talk into this thing like a telephone; the string had to be free to vibrate and to distort the magnetic flux.

'Many times in 1930 and 1931 we would take a piece of paper and some filings from the grinder and put a magnet under there and watch those filings dance around like they do. We'd study the flux patterns. I thought, why not go up there, above the magnet, and break the flux with the string itself? That was different from the Rickenbacker pickup, which wrapped around the strings on both the top and bottom. You don't see that kind today. My pickup was patented in [John's brother] Rudy Dopyera's name, because I worked for the corporation. It was plenty hard to get jobs in those days, so we all worked together and we didn't care whose name the patent was in.

'There were no other electric guitars on the market when the first electric Dobro came out, although people were doing things like sticking a microphone in front of a guitar or sticking one inside it. Now, you're going to hear that Rickenbacker was there first, or at least I've heard it, but we were there first. I don't know when their patent was done, but we were on the market first.'

As you can see, whether the Frying Pan predated Victor Smith's electric Dobro is disputed. Perhaps it did. Still, at the very least, the Frying Pan was the first electric to be built on a major scale for more than a few years, and thus remains nothing less than a milestone.

Epiphone and Gibson weigh in | The Epiphone Company of New York grew out of the House of Stathopoulo, which dated back to 1873. The founder's son, Epaminondas ('Epi') Stathopoulo, took over the company's presidency, lending his name to some of the instruments and finally renaming the company Epiphone. During the '30s, no other major manufacturer had a better reputation, and Epiphone's finest instruments were compared to the best Gibsons and even the creations of renowned luthiers like Elmer Stromberg and John

D'Angelico. (Although designed as acoustic guitars, Strombergs and D'Angelicos could be equipped with pickups, and the electrified models rank among the most acclaimed of all jazz-style guitars.)

By November 1935 the earliest Epiphone electrics, designed by salesman/inventor Herb Sunshine, had appeared under the Electar name. A December 1936 ad promoted the $100 Electar Hawaiian guitar with its amplifier in the case, an arrangement that would be reintroduced by Danelectro in the '50s. (In fact, it was Herb Sunshine who commissioned Nathan Daniel to build Epiphone's amplifiers; Daniel later founded Danelectro.)

Gibson claimed the electric guitar among its many inventions, and there were reportedly a few electric Spanish models built in the factory during the '20s. But they were prototypes (if they existed at all), and Lloyd Loar's electrics were never put into production by Gibson. In fact, there were no electric models in the line until three years or so after Loar had introduced his Vivi-Tones and three or four years after Dobro and Rickenbacker had introduced their electrics on a commercial scale.

Once Gibson entered the fray, however, it lent the new instrument incalculable legitimacy and prestige. Unlike Vivi-Tone, a one-man show, Gibson was a commercial powerhouse; unlike the California companies, it was steeped in decades of rich guitar heritage, that European tradition of guild craftsmen tapping away with hand tools. Gibson's imprimatur on the notion of amplification seemed to confirm, once and for all, that electric instruments were not just for Californians in Hawaiian shirts who played metal guitars etched with palm trees, or hillbillies who twanged hound-dog guitars with unsightly metal discs screwed into the top. No, the electric guitar was for pop players, too, even jazz players. Serious musicians. Artists! It was here to stay.

Like Rickenbacker, Gibson entered the electric market with a lap instrument. A flier dated 17 January 1936, announced the Gibson Electric Hawaiian guitar (there was no other model name), a six-string with a cobalt-magnet straight bar pickup. The matching EH150 four-stage, six-tube amp was a boxy, 15-Watt unit covered in 'aeroplane cloth' and featuring a 10-inch 'High Fidelity Ultrasonic Reproducer' (also known as a speaker). The guitar/amp combo cost $150

Opposite: George Beauchamp, co-inventor of the Frying Pan
Above: maverick inventor Lloyd Loar in his workshop
Inset: Vivi-Tone acoustic-electric with drawer-mounted pickup

and was soon dubbed the EH150 set. Gibson's 1936 catalogue contained much bigger news: the arch-top ES150, the Michigan company's debut electric Spanish guitar and the first of many Gibson landmarks in electric guitar design. The single pickup, later nicknamed the Charlie Christian (after the seminal jazzer who favoured the ES150) was designed by Walt Fuller; it was pointed at both ends and featured a chromed bar polepiece.

The fancier ES250, which followed, cost twice as much and demonstrated Gibson's increasing commitment to expanding the series. Other examples of Gibson electrics in the next several years included the ES300, with the company's first individually adjustable-polepiece pickup; the ES125; an electrified L7 (with its lead exiting the pickup unit itself, on top of the body); the Electraharp (the first pedal steel, designed by machinist John Moore and introduced in 1940); and electric versions of Gibson mandolins, tenor guitars, and banjos.

1936 was a big year for America's new instrument. Along with Gibson, at least two other manufacturers entered the market with their own models that year: Chicago's Kay, which unveiled a $95 guitar in January, and Vega of Boston, which in the following month announced its Electrovox guitar. The Aloha company had been established the year before in Chicago and was presumably selling its electric guitars and amplifiers by this time (under both the Aloha and Raleigh brands). Charles 'Chuck' Rubovits was once the president of Harmony, at one time the largest guitar manufacturer in the world. He told me, 'We were into electrics by 1938 with some Hawaiian models that had a pickup we bought from Rickenbacker. That was the early days of electrics, I'll tell you. That was long before Fender had a dream.'

Les and Leo | There were other individuals and companies building electric instruments prior to the Second World War, but it was primarily the guitars of Kalamazoo and Southern California that set the stage for the post-war explosion in electric guitar design, the most important aspect of which was the birth of the modern solidbody. Among the inventors and visionaries of guitar manufacturing in the first decades of the post-war era, two unassuming names would tower above all others: Les, and Leo. Les Paul's first stage name was

Top: Les Paul with Gibson president Ted McCarty
in the Gibson factory, circa 1956
Above: Les Paul and Mary Ford on the Ed Sullivan Show;
Les is using a heavily-modified Epiphone

Rhubarb Red, and under that handle he became something of a radio star in the 1920s. He hit Chicago in the early 1930s, playing jazz under his own name, and by that time he was already a tireless experimenter and savvy modifier of equipment. 'Once I jammed my mother's phonograph needle right into the top of a guitar and hooked it up,' he told me. 'It worked! I had my first electric. The Larson Brothers in Chicago made me an experimental model in 1934 with a maple top and no soundholes. "You're crazy," they said. "It won't vibrate." "I know it won't vibrate," I told 'em. "That's the whole idea." ' Like Lloyd Loar before him and Leo Fender after him, Les wanted to reproduce string vibrations without interference from the body's acoustic resonance; he was on his way to his first solidbody.

In 1936, Paul Barth made another guitar according to Les's specifications. Les himself fashioned one 'guitar' out of a railroad rail, of all things, and another from aluminium. Other experiments included an inexpensive Gibson arch-top modified for Les by the legendary John D'Angelico. Epi Stathopoulo was one of Les's many pals (an irrepressible raconteur, Les has friends literally around the globe), and he gave Les full access to Epiphone's factory. In 1941, at Epiphone, Les built what came to be known as The Log, a 4'' x 4'' board with strings, a pickup, and necessary hardware. 'I stuck on a regular guitar body for looks,' explained Les. 'Epi and his guys took one look and said, "Gee, this guy's strange!" '

Over the next several years Les pioneered many techniques now taken for granted in modern recording, such as echo, flanging, sound on sound, reverb, and multi-track itself. He continued to build radical guitars, and in about late 1949 he took The Log to the office of Maurice Berlin, who ran Chicago Musical Instruments, Gibson's parent company. 'I was a dyed-in-the-wool Gibson man, still am – and I showed it to Mr Berlin. He said, "Forget it." He called it a broomstick.' About two-and-a-half years later, after the success of Fender's early solidbodies, Mr Berlin would say to an aide, 'Find the kid with the broomstick. Sign him up.'

Nashville dealer George Gruhn recently uncovered a fascinating solidbody Spanish guitar that was marketed by the Slingerland drum company way back in 1938 or 1939. As Gruhn explains, 'This thing precedes The Log, all the Fender guitars, Bigsby's guitars, just about everything. It did not precede the Rickenbacker solidbody Spanish guitar, but while the Rick had a not-very-playable bakelite neck with "bumps" on it instead of real frets, this Slingerland is quite playable, with a wooden neck with actual frets. Also, the Rickenbacker had cavities in its bakelite body, but this is a true solidbody. The pickup has six coils, one for each string – it's pretty powerful. And this wasn't some prototype; it appeared in a published catalogue.'

Leo Fender was born in a barn on the family farm near Anaheim, California, in

1. Rickenbacker electric bass, circa 1936
2. Rickenbacker Electro Model B bakelite lap steel – its sister model Electro Spanish was the world's first solidbody electric
3. Rickenbacker endorsee Perry Botkin with the Vibrola Spanish electric. This electrified vibrato system, designed by Doc Kauffman, made the guitar so heavy it had to be mounted on a stand
4. Rickenbacker factory, circa 1936. At this time the company supplied resonators and pickups to other guitar manufacturers, including National

1909. Always interested in tools and gear, he built an acoustic guitar when he was a teenager and began working on pickups in the '30s. In the '40s, he went into business with the late Clayton 'Doc' Kauffman, who had come to California from a Kansas farm in 1922 and played various instruments in local country bands around Orange County.

Doc and Leo were alike in several respects – neither could look at a piece of gear without trying to figure out some way to improve it. Doc had fashioned steam engines from five-gallon milk cans when he was a teenager and went on to build farm machinery, power tools, police transmitters – even a motorcycle. A half-century later, Doc's house and shop remained cluttered with gizmos and gadgets in various stages of completion.

In August 1929, Doc had patented one of the very earliest vibrato tailpieces, perhaps the first. Nine years later he designed a motor-driven vibrato that wiggled the tailpiece; both patents were assigned to Electro. He also claimed to be the first person to install amplifier components in the top of the cabinet, the way it's done on most amps today, simply to avoid the trouble of having to bend over to make adjustments. (No task was too small for Doc's attention. He took me for a ride in his car one time; sitting in the driver's seat, he whipped out a wooden rod with a tip that he'd modified to fit the door locks, so that he could unlock the passenger door without having to stretch. 'Saves my back,' he explained.)

'Leo came in one day,' Doc recounted, 'and said, "Hey, you've been building guitars around here – do you want to build some together?" And I said, "Well, sure, sounds okay to me." ' Calling their company K&F, Kauffman and Fender began building small amps and lap steels. While the pair were constructing their first industrial gas oven, the guitars were baked in the Kauffman family's kitchen stove.

'I had seen Doc in the middle 1930s,' Leo told me in 1978. 'He used to play instorefronts to draw a little business for the store and also to sign up a few students for himself. We were in business until about February of 1946. K&F began to take up so much of an investment that Doc got worried. He thought he'd better get out while he had a full skin. Fender Electric Instruments grew out of K&F. I just continued the thing and expanded it and changed the name.'

As Doc explained, 'I told myself I'd never go into debt for anything. Leo was different – he'd go into debt on an investment like a house afire! He's a pursuer, boy, day and night! That's what put the guitar where it is.'

Another fixture on the Southern California guitar scene of the late '40s was Paul Bigsby, a close pal of Country guitar giant Merle Travis. One day Travis sketched a radical guitar shape on a radio station programme sheet and poked it across the table to Bigsby. 'Can you build me this thing?' 'I can build anything!' responded Paul, with a characteristic loud laugh. The resulting instrument, a solidbody Spanish model, became one of guitar history's most controversial pieces, for Merle claimed that the idea for the Fender's earliest guitar – the first modern commercial solidbody Spanish guitar and thus one of the most important instruments ever conceived – was taken from the Bigsby that he designed. On more than one occasion, Merle stated that Leo Fender came to a gig one night to see the guitar and actually borrowed it for a week, returning with his own hastily built instrument. 'I designed the Fender guitar, you know,' Merle told *Guitar Player* magazine in 1976, 'and Paul Bigsby built the first one.'

Leo Fender disagreed, quietly but utterly. Both he and Merle recounted with impressive conviction and detail the time when Fender first saw Travis's Bigsby, but the stories vary considerably in the particulars and especially in the implication. Fender stated that he never borrowed the Bigsby and, more important, that his own guitar (later to be called the Telecaster) had been designed well in advance of his first seeing it.

Merle Travis's Bigsby had a body shaped somewhat like Gibson's Les Paul (not introduced until 1952) and a headstock shaped undeniably like Fender's Stratocaster of 1954. Regarding the basic idea of a solidbody electric Spanish guitar, it's virtually impossible that Leo would have got the idea from the Bigsby, since solidbodies had been marketed for years by Vivi-Tone and Rickenbacker, and the latter was right there in Orange County – Leo Fender's back yard. Furthermore, Leo recounted that in 1943 or 1944, he had a 'standard' (meaning Spanish, as opposed to a lap model) electric guitar of his own design that he used to rent to local musicians. 'Doc did a lot of the work on it,' Leo explained. 'It was an extreme cutaway – didn't look anything like the Fender guitars.' There is no reason to doubt that Fender and Travis, like other prominent figures before and since, could have been working independently on similar ideas. At the very least, Merle Travis sketched the headstock silhouette that became a world-famous Fender hallmark five or six years before it appeared on any Fender.

Whatever its ultimate influence, the guitar that Paul Bigsby built for the first Travis picker was remarkably modern, especially when compared to Vivi-Tone's

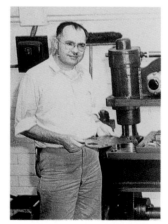

1   2   3

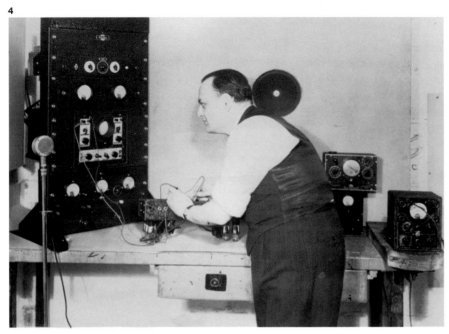

board-body guitars or Rickenbacker's noncutaway Spanish solidbodies, which resembled baritone ukuleles. (And certainly, Paul Bigsby's spring-operated hand vibrato, available on guitars from Gibson, Silvertone, Gretsch, Guild, and many more, was perhaps the pre-eminent mechanical guitar accessory of the 1950s and early 1960s.) The Bigsby/Travis guitar's destiny, like that of Les Paul's Log and others, was to be one of those instruments whose historical significance derived not from their evolutionary influence but rather from their exalted but commercially untenable status of being ahead of their time.

With the '40s drawing to a close, there were plenty of electric guitars to choose from, with established companies like Gibson, Harmony, Kay, National Dobro (the two had merged in 1935), Rickenbacker, and Epiphone solidly behind the concept. Gretsch had entered the field, tentatively at first. England's James Ormston Burns had already built his first electric Hawaiian guitar and would soon introduce his first solidbody Spanish model. Hawaiian-style guitarist and radio performer Lowell Kiesel had moved to Los Angeles, where in 1946 he established the Carvin company (named after two of his sons, Carson and Gavin). By 1948 Nat Daniel had established Danelectro and was building amplifiers and echo units in his Red Bank, New Jersey, plant, and Gibson and DeArmond were offering retrofit pickups that could electrify practically any acoustic.

As America and the rest of the world looked forward to the '50s, the electric guitar seemed to be comfortably entrenched. Still, no one foresaw the explosion in its popularity that would accompany the development of the modern solidbody and invention of the electric bass by Leo Fender, the rise of a new kind of music called rock'n'roll, and a transatlantic musical phenomenon that would come to be called the 'British invasion'.

1. The Bigsby/Travis guitar – did it inspire Leo to make his own solidbody electric?
2. Leo Fender, the Henry Ford of the electric guitar
3. Early K&F lap steel
4. Inventor and salesman, Herb Sunshine of Epiphone
5. Early Epiphone bar pickup; compare it to the 'Charlie Christian' pickup, page 17

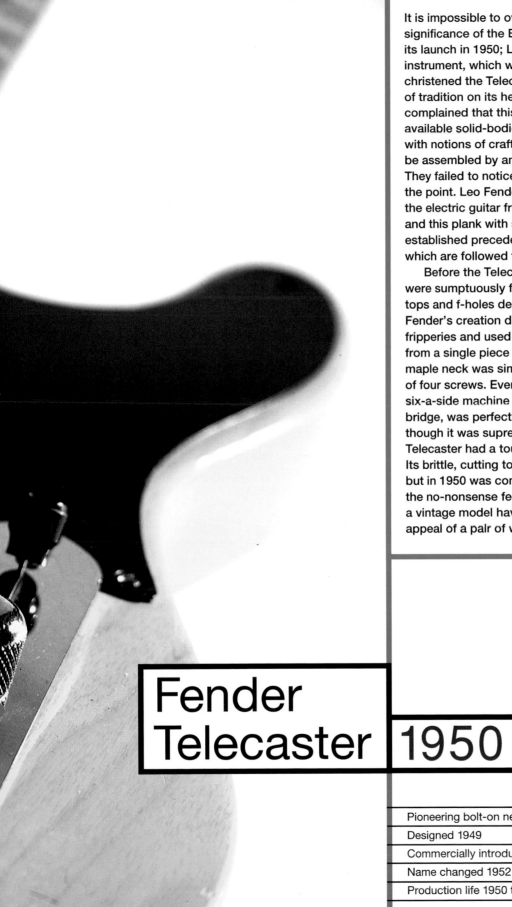

It is impossible to overstate the significance of the Broadcaster on its launch in 1950; Leo Fender's new instrument, which would soon be re-christened the Telecaster, turned centuries of tradition on its head. Fender's rivals complained that this, the first commercially available solid-bodied guitar, dispensed with notions of craftsmanship, and could be assembled by any idiot with a bandsaw. They failed to notice that this was exactly the point. Leo Fender had re-considered the electric guitar from first principles, and this plank with six strings attached established precedents in guitar-making which are followed to this day.

Before the Telecaster, electric guitars were sumptuously finished, with carved tops and f-holes derived from violins; Fender's creation dispensed with these fripperies and used a solid body made from a single piece of ash, while the all-maple neck was simply attached by means of four screws. Every other detail, from the six-a-side machine heads to the adjustable bridge, was perfectly considered. But even though it was supremely practical, the Telecaster had a touch of magic about it. Its brittle, cutting tone is distinctive today, but in 1950 was completely unique, while the no-nonsense feel and construction of a vintage model have the brute blue-collar appeal of a pair of well-worn Levis.

Fender
Telecaster | 1950

Pioneering bolt-on neck solid body electric
Designed 1949
Commercially introduced 1950
Name changed 1952
Production life 1950 to date

The individual components of the Broadcaster were not unique; nor was the concept of a solid-bodied Spanish (as opposed to lap steel) guitar a totally new one – the solid-bodied Paul Bigsby/Merle Travis guitar was similar in concept, while Rickenbacker had a bakelite solid body model in production by 1935. Leo Fender's real genius lay in making use of these concepts in an instrument which was simple and optimized for mass production, yet which was sufficiently versatile to give it a production life which has now exceeded 40 years.

The construction of the guitar may be considered prosaic today, but was groundbreaking at its launch. The solid slab body was the epitome of minimalism, while the neck was simply attached by four screws (and invariably termed 'bolt-on'). This neck was more suited to mass production than the conventional glued-in equivalent, and easier to replace in the event of damage. The controls were mounted on a chrome strip, mounted to the top of the guitar and attached by two screws. This provided electrical screening, straightforward maintenance, and once again was optimized for mass production. A black phenolic plastic scratchplate (black fibre on early models) protected the body from over-zealous strummers, and concealed the mounting screws of the chrome-covered rhythm pickup.

The bridge plate was a simply stamped piece of metal, but was advanced for its time by providing adjustable intonation for the strings, in three pairs, enabling more accurate tuning when playing up the neck. The treble pickup was slanted, to give a sharper sound to the top strings, and was mounted on the bridge plate by three screws. The strings were simply anchored at the back of the body by six chromed ferrules.

1   2

Gibson's guitars of the time were assembled by craftsmen; each guitar required complicated routing and gluing, and on instruments such as Gibson's best-selling ES175 mounting or replacing the electrical hardware was extremely complicated. On the Broadcaster, however, all the routing was performed from the top of the instrument, with the exception of that for the output jack, which was mounted on the edge of the guitar, once again on a chrome plate. These factors made the guitar more durable, easier to repair and simpler to produce.

The neck's all-maple construction again defied tradition. Most existing guitars had a glued on fingerboard, with a channel for the truss rod underneath. On the Broadcaster the truss rod was inserted from the back of the neck, with the routed channel filled by a 'skunk stripe' of dark walnut. This was done for aesthetic reasons, as Leo liked the idea of the guitar's 'all blonde' look. Some guitarists feel that the resulting one-piece neck, with the frets mounted directly on the front, sounds better than the conventional construction; functionally

'It's amazing when you think that Leo invented the Telecaster back in 1950 and got it right first time. I'm like a **plumber with his favourite wrench –** they do the job and I swear by them!'

Keith Richards

Telecaster 1950

3

Main shot: Fender Broadcaster circa 1950
1. The string retainer on the headstock prevents top strings popping out of nut
2. Headstock face is flush with the body – a major change from the conventional practice of back-angled headstocks
3. The Broadcaster/Tele used a bolt-on neck construction previously only used with banjos

it was not a great improvement on the standard method – Fender would later introduce glued on rosewood and maple fingerboards.

The guitar's headstock was, once again, unique in production terms, although it possessed some similarities to the Bigsby/Travis guitar. Most importantly, it established the precedent of having the strings pass directly over the nut to the tuning machines, without being splayed at an angle, as on most Gibson guitars. This minimized friction at the nut and helped improve tuning stability, while the slot head design of the tightly-packed Kluson tuners helped lock the strings securely in place.

Even now, the sound of the world's first production solid body stands up against modern guitars. Testing a 1952 Telecaster, rewired to give the later pickup switching, revealed an awesome sound and playing feel that stands up to the most expensive modern production instruments. The guitar weighs only 7 1/2lb (3.4kg), considerably lighter than many modern copies or reissues, and the bridge pickup, in particular, has a ringing attack which is unequalled even today, but has a body to

the tone which is missing from '70s models – and Japanese copies. By comparison the neck pickup sounds soft, but again quite full, while the Tele's only real practical drawback is a tendency to microphony and noise pickup. Today the Telecaster's taut and crisp sound has become the standard for rhythm guitar, as perhaps best exemplified by Keith Richards, while it is also perfect for stinging Country lead lines as practised by James Burton or Roy Buchanan. Both sounds have become almost ubiquitous in modern music; it's to Leo's credit that while most of the instrument contemporaries only have appeal as period pieces, even early Teles are still in regular use by musicians as diverse as Francis Rossi and Bruce Springsteen.

But Leo's first work did stop short of perfection. Although the Broadcaster was a pioneering example of a two pickup guitar, one positioned near the fingerboard for a mellow sound, and one near the bridge for a cutting, clear sound, the early pickup switching was eccentric, without the option of both pickups on at once. The switching would eventually change to a conventional either or both pickup arrangement. It was also impossible to adjust the rhythm pickup's height without removing the scratchplate – an inconvenience that still applies to many modern copies; adjusting the truss rod, too, required the scratchplate's removal.

Leo provided a flashy chrome cover for the bridge, which helped provide magnetic screening but interfered with guitarists' ability to mute strings at the bridge with the palm of their hands; the cover, therefore, was generally converted to use as an ash tray.

Lastly, Fender used a name for the guitar that belonged to guitar and drum makers Gretsch – they had a kit called the Broadkaster, and threatened a law suit. In keeping with the much-touted new age of television, the guitar's name was changed to Telecaster in mid 1952.

The Telecaster's bridge is one of the major factors in the guitar's distinctive sound. At the time of the guitar's introduction the unit had real advantages over its rivals; now it looks bizarrely primitive, a simple piece of stamped steel with three brass bridge saddles attached. When Leo designed the Broadcaster, as it was first known, the guitar's adjustable bridge saddles were unique, allowing string height and intonation to be adjusted, in three pairs. The method of anchoring the strings was also novel – previously all production electric guitars had featured a separate tailpiece. Typically for Fender, the arrangement was the simplest one that would do the job.

Various improved versions of the Tele bridge have been produced, with heavier cast baseplates or six separate bridge saddles as on the example shown here (a mirror placed underneath shows the pickup's grounding plate).

The Telecaster's bridge unit is unique in that it also comprises the mounting plate for the bridge pickup; this, together with the copper grounding plate fitted underneath the pickup on early models, is one of the main causes of the Telecaster's uniquely biting sound. The pickup is in direct physical contact with the strings and the whole assembly is, quite literally, microphonic; tapping the assembly with the guitar plugged in produces a clear sound from the amplifier. Later Telecastors, which dispensed with the grounding plate and moved to heavier bridge assemblies, were less susceptible to squealing feedback, but lost some of the characteristic Tele bite.

Telecaster 1950

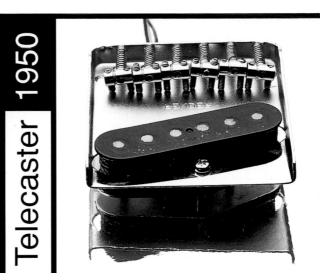

Left: 1952 Telecaster: apart from the new name, this guitar and the Broadcaster pictured are almost identical
4. This modern US-built '52 reissue goes all out to replicate the original model
5. The modern Telecaster is remarkably unchanged from the original. This '92 US Standard Telecaster features 'hotter' pickups with a humbucker in bridge position

4

5

In 1949 Gibson enjoyed a comfortable position, dominating the market for arch-top and electric guitars. For the 15 years in which the electric guitar had been in existence Gibson chose to ignore the gimmickry to which its competitors often resorted, concentrating on well-made professional instruments. The ES175 epitomized that tradition, but acknowledged the new pre-eminence of the electric guitar.

Designed as an electric from the ground up, rather than an acoustic with a pickup added, Gibson's new instrument was intended as the company's premier mass market electric, keenly priced at only $175.

In production ever since, the ES175 boasts the longest continuous production run of any electric guitar. But although this deep bodied, reassuringly traditional instrument epitomizes Gibson's heritage, it also helped usher in an era of mass production instruments which would fundamentally change the nature of Gibson as a company.

Gibson ES175 | 1949

The 'longest running' electric guitar

Designed 1948-1949

Commercially introduced 1949

Production life 1949 to date

Although often typecast as traditionalist, Gibson, more than any other company, dominated the pre-war electric guitar market – their ES150 had been by far the most popular electric of the '30s. The Second World War caused a brief hiatus in the company's expansion, but when the company was purchased by the Chicago Musical Instrument Corporation, headed by Maurice Berlin, in 1944, Berlin correctly foresaw that there would be a huge post-war expansion in demand for the guitar. Berlin recruited Theodore – or 'Ted' – McCarty from the Wurlitzer organ company in 1948, and groomed him to become the company president within 18 months. McCarty recalls that those early years saw strong pressures to keep producing new models, and the 1948-1950 period saw the launch of the ES350 – Gibson's first major electric cutaway guitar – the three pickup ES5, the budget model ES125 and the lavish Super 400C. Although the company's acoustic arch-tops like the budget-model L-50, were selling well in the post-war period, Gibson concentrated their efforts on the electric sector. The ES175 was to prove this a wise move.

The construction of the ES175 was entirely traditional. Although earlier Gibsons featured hand-carved arch-tops usually made of spruce, this lower priced model used a pressed ply top, as on the earlier, pricier ES350. The shape, mainly designed by Gibson's workshop team headed by Larry Allers and John Huis, featured twin f-holes and a single Florentine (sharp) cutaway. Gibson's founder, Orville Gibson, had designed a single cutaway guitar in the 1900s, but it was the 350 and 175 that helped this cutaway shape become an industry standard.

The ES175's construction is typical Gibson; the sides are made of solid maple, with the pressed maple ply front and back attached by a kerfed mahogany lining. The neck is made of one piece of mahogany with a bound rosewood fingerboard and attaches to the body via a large maple block,

1

'I've bought a lot of guitars I didn't need – **I'm selling 45 at the moment** – **but I've kept my '63 175,** which was actually the first Gibson I ever bought. I played it continuously for 15 years, until Close To The Edge' *Steve Howe*

while the headstock is of typical Gibson back-angled three-a-side design, with the truss rod accessed by a bell-shaped plate above the nut. The guitar features a simple trapeze tailpiece to angle the strings, which pass over a simple height adjustable rosewood bridge held in place by string pressure.

On its launch the ES175 featured a single P90 pickup, with one volume and one tone control. This single-coil design, at the time Gibson's main pickup, featured adjustable polepieces and wide, shallow windings, giving quite a fat sound in comparison with other single-coil pickups. Later models of ES175 featured new fittings as they were developed by Gibson; a double pickup model was launched in 1953, while the guitar gained humbucking pickups and a metal tune-o-matic bridge in 1957.

Playing an original 1949 example demonstrates just how different Gibson's mainline electric was from Leo Fender's Broadcaster of the following year. The guitar exudes craftsmanship, and although simple is extremely well-made, belying its budget origins. Despite the single-coil pickup, the sound is fat and well rounded, and the feel of the fingerboard is extremely

comfortable; more so than the body itself, which at 3 3/8" in depth is unwieldy, while the bulky neck fitting inhibits access to the higher frets, despite the cutaway. Generally categorized as a jazzer's guitar, the ES175 does in fact excel in this role, offering a fat woody tone which is good for juicy jazz chords, but does not stretch to sustained lead lines – the guitar is also prone to feedback at higher volumes.

Given that the ES175 possesses most of the virtues of Gibson's existing electrics, but at a fraction of the price, it's not surprising that the guitar almost immediately became one of the company's best selling electric guitars, outsold only by the company's lower-priced ES125 range. Ironically, however, the ES175 was the end of an era. The ES175 was a large factor in rendering the electric guitar ubiquitous in jazz circles, selling over 1200 examples in a single year – but that total, impressive at the time, would be dwarfed by Gibson's solid body sales as rock'n'roll took hold in the late '50s. Yet as other designs came and went, the ES175 has had the last laugh, surviving its newer rivals as they went in and out of fashion. Still a current Gibson model, the ES175 boasts the longest continuous period in production of any electric guitar.

Main shot: The ES175 was resolutely traditional, but offered superb value for money
1. Both front and back are made of pressed ply
2. Back-angled headstock is typical of Gibson designs
3. The ES175 featured the then-standard Gibson P90 pickup, replaced by humbuckers in 1957

The '50s:

Rock'n'Roll Music!

It was the establishment's ultimate nightmare. At the beginning of the century Karl Marx had advocated giving the workers control of the means of production. Now, horror of horrors, the electric guitar gave the kids control of the means of making music!

Although big band music had, by the '40s, produced 'bobby sox' idols of the likes of Bing Crosby and Frank Sinatra, actual control of the music was invested in the hands of bandleaders who had the experience and financial means to support a whole team of musicians. The electric guitar meant that aspiring musicians could pick up an instrument and assemble a band within a matter of months. As a result, the face of popular music was to change for ever.

The technology required for rock'n'roll was all in place by 1948. The electric guitar was readily available, as Gibson expanded its mid-price models and companies like Harmony and Kay introduced budget-priced electrics. As recording and broadcasting equipment became more affordable, independent radio stations and record companies proliferated, dedicated to the 'race' music that was ignored by larger concerns.

Jazz music forms had become highly developed by the '40s; works like Duke Ellington's 'Creole Rhapsody' were sophisticated in composition and arrangement; by comparison blues and western forms were primitive, although Louis Jordan in particular developed a sophisticated form of jump blues that appealed to both black and white audiences and was a major catalyst in the development of rhythm and blues. Between 1945 and 1955, however, both blues and western forms – and electric guitar-playing – developed rapidly.

In the blues field, musicians such as Muddy Waters and Howlin' Wolf amplified the music of the Mississippi delta, drawing on the legacy of the legendary Robert Johnson. Johnson himself was a fiendish guitarist and composer who had laid much of the groundwork for Chicago blues with songs like 'Dust My Broom' and 'Love In Vain'. It's often rumoured that Johnson experimented with an electric guitar and a band backing, and was therefore on the point of creating what we now know as Chicago blues before the Second World War. Johnson's death in August 1938, after drinking whisky poisoned by a jealous husband, meant it would be Waters who changed Delta blues from a solo, rustic format to a powerful, electrified band-based sound. Meanwhile guitarists like Lowell Fulson (on the West Coast) and B.B. King (based in Memphis Tennessee) expanded on the sophisticated lead guitar style of T-Bone Walker.

In Country music, guitarists like Ernest Tubbs were using electric guitars by the early '40s, while Merle Travis perfected a distinctly electric guitar sound, damping his strings with the palm of his right hand – a technique which would also go on to inspire Chet Atkins. Western swing bands such as Bob Wills And His Texas Playboys employed a distinctly electric sound, and boasted a string of celebrated electric guitarists including Eldon Shamblin, Jimmy Wyble and Lester 'Junior' Barnard. Wills himself accentuated the blues influences that had always been present in Country and hillbilly music; his style was a heavy influence on William Haley, a one-time yodelling cowboy who formed a western swing combo – The Saddlemen – and started playing black R&B songs. When Bill Haley re-named his band the Comets, signed to Decca and recruited Louis Jordan's old producer, Milt Gabler, he became the world's first rock'n'roll hero. Essentially, Haley's music was identical to the R&B on which it was modelled – but it was aimed at a white audience, a concept first grasped by Alan Freed, who started his 'Moondog Rock'n'Roll Party' radio show in June 1951.

But although rock'n'roll might have started as R&B bought by whites, it would soon evolve into something entirely distinct. The first sign of this was Jackie Brenston's 'Rocket 88', recorded in 1951 by independent producer Sam Phillips. The making of 'Rocket 88' is a classic rock'n'roll story, set on the classic rock'n'roll thoroughfare – Highway 61. A young piano-playing Ike Turner, vocalist Brenston and the five band members overloaded their car on the journey to Phillips' studio in Memphis. Willie Kizart's hefty valve guitar amp fell off the car's roof, and when the band arrived in the studio they found that a damaged speaker gave his guitar a fuzzy, distorted tone. Phillips, who was contracted to produce the session for the Chicago Chess label, decided to go with the sound, and in the process created what was probably the first rock'n'roll record ever, and the first 'purposefully' distorted guitar on record. The record became a Number One R&B hit for Chess, and was later covered by Bill Haley.

Clockwise from bottom left
Chuck Berry: From Hank Williams to neighbourhood blues, he could do it all
Bo Diddley (centre) models the ultimate rock star accoutrements of custom Gretsch and custom scooter
James Burton, star of the Telecaster, here seen with an early Fender six-string bass

From 1954, early rock'n'roll hits followed a variety of formats; Haley's music was a combination of sax-based western swing and jump blues. Fats Domino trailblazed for New Orleans piano-based R&B, while vocal groups such as The Coasters or Frankie Lymon and the Teenagers presaged a move to anodyne schmaltz that would kill off rock'n'roll by 1960. But two other formats would finally unleash the power of small electric combos and create the basis for all of today's rock music: Country rock, or rockabilly, and Chicago R&B, the foremost examples of which were Elvis Presley and Chuck Berry.

Rockabilly Rebels

Although Elvis Presley might now be regarded as the perfect symbol of America's overconsumption and moral slovenliness, his inspired re-working of Arthur Crudup's 1946 hit 'That's All Right Mama' rendered him beyond criticism for all eternity. Like all great records, 'That's All Right...' transcended its genre, a synthesis of hillbilly music and Delta blues, and incidentally dispensed with the need for Bill Haley. Presley interpreted R&B without watering it down, while Sam Phillips co-ordinated the perfect rock production, punctuated by Scotty Moore's economical guitar riffs.

Other white musicians followed Presley's lead; Eddie Cochran was an expert Country session player, whose songs were written around simple, crisply amplified riffs – Cochran modified his Gretsch 6120 electric with a Gibson P90 pickup to obtain a classic electric sound that would later heavily influence The Who. Buddy Holly utilized the new Fender Stratocaster to explore a similar cocktail of blues and western influences. Like Presley and Cochran, Holly's arrangements used the electric guitar and vocal as the main elements of simple instrumentation; the guitar would typically open the song with a simple riff and then trade with the vocal melody throughout the song. The rhythm section would generally consist of just bass and drums, which, in Holly's case, would often be stripped down to merely a pair of tom toms – or even a pair of slapped thighs...

All of these electric combos were exploring the use of electronic effects, an avenue first explored by Les Paul in the late '40s. Holly double tracked his voice for songs like 'Words of Love', while Phillips used slapback tape echo as an integral part of all of Sun's records. Duane Eddy, who enjoyed a series of hits produced by Lee Hazelwood, starting with 'Movin' and Groovin'' in 1958, reflected the spirit of experimentation of the time: 'We had three tracks to play with, and a brand new thing called stereo. We were recording out in Phoenix Arizona, and we used a big five hundred gallon tank as an echo chamber. We set up a mike in one end and a speaker in the other, and we had to go out in the morning and chase the birds off the tank so they wouldn't chirrup their way through the songs. If a fire engine came along we'd have to stop playing – we lost a lot of good takes that way!'

Dale Hawkins's 'Suzie Q' was perhaps the archetypal '50s guitar record. It revolved almost entirely around the guitar skills of James Burton, whose fiery rhythm lick and scorching solo probably amounted to the first use of a heavily amplified electric outside the blues field:

'Right from when I was a little kid I'd listen to the radio a lot, to people like Merle Travis and Chet Atkins – Chet was one of my idols. But I got into listening to a lot of blues players like Elmore James or Lightnin' Hopkins – it was the same music to me.' Burton was one of the first guitarists to experiment with light gauge strings. 'I was listening to a lot of blues records and the way they'd get the vibrato sound with a slide guitar. I thought there had to be a way to do it with a regular guitar, and thought maybe that if the string was lighter you could do this without breaking your fingers! So I went and got some banjo strings, put them on the fifth and sixth strings, then worked out if I used four guitar strings and moved them down – used an A string for the E, and a D string for the A – it was perfect!' Light gauge strings meant that a guitarist could bend notes or add vibrato far more easily; the idea would later be marketed by companies like Ernie Ball, and similar gauges to the ones Burton used would become standard.

Roll Over Beethoven

Johnnie Johnson was a piano player who led a trio playing standards at the Cosmopolitan Club in Illinois. On New Year's Eve, 1952, his sax player fell ill.

'I'd met Chuck when we were playing the same clubs in St Louis so I called him in to sit with us. When he started to sing a hillbilly number, the crowd went half crazy. They took to him so well that we just hung on in there.'

Chuck Berry had taken up the guitar planning to emulate T-Bone Walker, or Carl Hogan from Louis Jordan's Tympany Five. Yet when he teamed up with Johnnie Johnson, later taking over leadership of Johnson's trio, Berry came up with a completely new hybrid. His guitar style seemed more related to boogie woogie piano playing than blues guitar – Keith Richards, Berry's most devoted acolyte, has suggested that Chuck took Johnson's riffs and transferred them to guitar. Much of Berry's material was effectively straight Country – 'It Don't Take But A Few Minutes', for instance, could have been recorded by Hank Williams.

Above: Buddy Holly was rock'n'roll's first
exponent of the Strat
Left: Young sex god Eddie Cochran
Below: Duane Eddy, at the Arizona
Recorders studio, 1958
Opposite: The electric bass was
becoming common in blues and
rock'n'roll circles by 1956-1957. This
1958 shot of Jerry Lee Lewis and band
shows Jay Brown with a
Fender Precision

'We had to go out in the morning and chase
the birds off the tank so they wouldn't chirrup
their way through the songs.

**If a fire engine came along we'd have to stop
playing – we lost a lot of good takes that way!'**
Duane Eddy

'I've always been some kind of a thick head, and it took me enough time learning the guitar without using different tunings.

I guess I was trying to get that sound, but with a normal guitar.'

Yet Berry also absorbed Latin influences and rhythms, wrote straightforward blues like 'In The Wee Wee Hours' – 'those were for the neighbourhood', played Hawaiian pedal steel on songs like 'Deep Feeling' (a dead ringer for Fleetwood Mac's 'Albatross') and wrote a string of teen anthems. Although Presley had the edge on Berry in terms of sex appeal – as well as the distinct advantage of being white – Berry was the prime mover in creating rock'n'roll, and created a blueprint for the beat and rock music that would succeed it. Berry's clear guitar sound, based on his Gibson ES350 and a Fender amplifier, used no frills or gimmicks, but provided the basis for his superb songwriting. Although Berry would attract hosts of imitators, most could not match the nuances of his style, which used subtle pairings of notes and a 'bright' major feel which owed more to Country than to the blues. Not for nothing did The Rolling Stones' Keith Richards comment that 'There was a time in my life where the only thing I wanted to do was to play guitar like Chuck Berry.'

Berry's label, Chess, attempted to repeat Berry's crossover appeal with their other artists. The only one who came close, however, was Bo Diddley. Diddley was a masterful performer – although his distinctive style was to ultimately prove limiting – who was an early experimenter in bizarre guitar sounds. His recordings used heavy fuzztones and tremolo effects, created by a device which Diddley claims to have made himself using clock parts! Diddley's aggressive approach and distinctive rhythms would later be copied by Buddy Holly, The Rolling Stones, The Animals, and many others...

Blues Horizons | Blues singer Muddy Waters never admitted to regretting the day he introduced Chuck Berry to Chess Records, even though his label mate's record sales put those of Chess stalwarts Waters, Sonny Boy Williamson and Howlin' Wolf in the shade. But while Berry was to hog the limelight, the Chicago blues scene which Waters represented would later prove a huge influence on popular music.

Waters discovered the power of electricity in the late '40s, as did Sonny Boy Williamson, who teamed up with Robert Nighthawk, a formidable guitarist who was playing the electric by 1940. Waters had been recorded by Library Of Congress archivist Alan Lomax in 1941, and was an authentic and earthy acoustic Delta blues

Opposite: A young B.B. King sports a Fender Esquire in this early '50s shot
Left: Howlin' Wolf – probably *the* heaviest bluesman of the decade

guitarist. By 1947 he was working as an electric guitarist with Sunnyland Slim for Chicago's Chess label (then trading as Aristocrat). By 1948 Waters had recorded new versions of 'I Can't Be Satisfied' and 'I Feel Like Going Home', two songs which had featured on his Library of Congress recordings. But his new style was unmistakably city-based, its electric nature giving his sound real presence and sustain. Released despite the misgivings of label proprietor Leonard Chess, the record's first pressing sold out in one day, and has come to be regarded by many as the first record in the style that is now known as 'Chicago blues'.

Although Chicago blues came directly from the Mississippi delta, elsewhere other guitarists were expanding on the legacy of T-Bone Walker. Lowell Fulson was one of the first. Groomed on sophisticated jazz and jump blues, he could also turn his hand to Country music when necessary. 'The one thing I always wanted to do was have a big band. I got an electric when I came out of the Navy after the war – that meant we could go out on the road with just a couple of saxophones – and we could make money, too!' Fulson enjoyed his first hit with 'Three O'Clock Blues' in 1948, a song which four years later also became a hit for B.B. King.

King, too, had a love for sophisticated big band music, as well as the highly technical guitar work of Lonnie Johnson. King was encouraged in his early days by his mother's cousin, Delta bluesman Bukka White. According to the self-deprecating King, 'I used to love the sound that you'd get from bottleneck guitar, but I've always been some kind of a thick head, and it took me enough time learning the guitar without using different tunings. I guess I was trying to get that sound, but with a normal guitar.'

But King learned fast. He started off playing an acoustic with a DeArmond pickup, and by his first recordings was using Gibson semi-acoustics. His early 78s display a variety of approaches – 1951's 'She's Dynamite', produced by Sam Phillips, shows him using a heavily distorted and gimmicky fuzztone, while on some mid '50s recordings he used a Fender Strat, giving a stingingly clear sound. But by 1958 King had bought the new Gibson 335 which with its combination of electric and acoustic properties suited his sound perfectly – as well as his girth! 'It was so comfortable to play, even back then when I was somewhat slimmer than I am now!' King perfected a synthesis of gospel and blues, with jazz influences, and expanded on T-Bone Walker's legacy with a combination of sustain and expressiveness that allowed him to trade vocal lines with his guitar. B.B. was also to prove a major influence on his two (non-related) namesakes, Albert and Freddie. Albert King, who moved to St Louis in 1956, played early support dates with B.B, and was to come into his own with superb blues/soul crossover material like 'Born Under A Bad Sign' for Stax in the mid '60s. Freddie King's early Federal recordings, such as his cover of B.B.'s 'Have You Ever Loved A Woman?', showed him strongly influenced by his namesake, but by 1960 Freddie's fiery style resulted in classics like 1960's 'Hideaway' and 1961's 'The Stumble', both of which were to prove a major influence on British blues guitarists such as Eric Clapton and Peter Green.

Throughout the '50s, Chess was America's premier blues label, and a mecca for aspiring guitarists. Howlin' Wolf's first recordings, in 1951, rank among the heaviest records made in that decade – guitarist Willie Johnson used a heavily distorted sound, which perfectly matched Wolf's rasping voice. Other Chess stalwarts included Jimmy Rogers, who played with Muddy Waters' regular band, Robert 'Junior' Lockwood and Hubert Sumlin – the latter an unpredictable player who emphasized the grainy eccentricity of Wolf's sound.

During the '50s, Chess acquired a 'house producer', Willie Dixon. Originally called in for his bass-playing skills, Dixon moved over to production with the advent of the electric bass, writing songs for all of Chess's major blues acts. Dixon had firm ideas about what constituted a commercial song: 'It had to have an introduction to start the song off. It had to have a different sound for it to go over, and different words that will catch in people's minds.' The result was a set of songs which relied on heavily-amplified guitar riffs, together with catchy story lines, thus subverting their 12-bar origins. Records like 'Little Red Rooster', '(I'm Your) Hoochie Coochie Man' and 'I Just Wanna Make Love To You' were blues hits that would become successful pop songs when covered by English bands, and would also provide a basis for heavy metal when recorded by

the likes of Led Zeppelin. Dixon was an astute talent spotter, bringing a young Buddy Guy and Otis Rush to Chess, both after short stints with rival labels.

Guy and Rush, who both started working for Chess in 1960, represented a new generation of guitarists. Guy had absorbed the influence of B.B. King, as well as the guitar sound of Guitar Slim, a New Orleans guitarist who had a hit in 1954 with 'The Things I Used To Do'. Slim's initial heavily-amplified sound was unfortunately watered down when the guitarist signed to the Atco label in 1956, and his premature death in 1959 meant he left only a small body of work. Guy was to pick up the baton, and although he experimented with a Les Paul until it was stolen, he was perhaps the first guitarist to really master the Fender Stratocaster. He paired the instrument with a very loud Fender Bassman, a bass amp which gave a smooth overdrive sound, and also made heavy use of the Strat's 'out of phase' in-between switch positions. He was also a natural showman: 'I was playing twice a week and getting seven dollars a night. But my rent was fifteen dollars a week so I had to get the money in tips.'

Guy had a 100-foot long guitar lead made up 'so I used to walk right into the audience where I could look at them face to face to see if they thought I was playing right. I was kinda excited in those days and had a lot of energy, so I used to get the tips. If I hadn't, I wouldn't be here now, cause it would be impossible for me to make fourteen dollars a week and pay out fifteen for that room...'

In many ways Guy represented the start-off point for Jimi Hendrix a few years later; Guy has claimed that he tried persuading Chess to record his heavily distorted style.

'When I was playing in clubs I used to have distortion, feedback, and the audiences used to love it. I told Leonard Chess we should get that sound on record, but he just told me "ain't nobody gonna buy that noise, man."'

Six years later, they would.

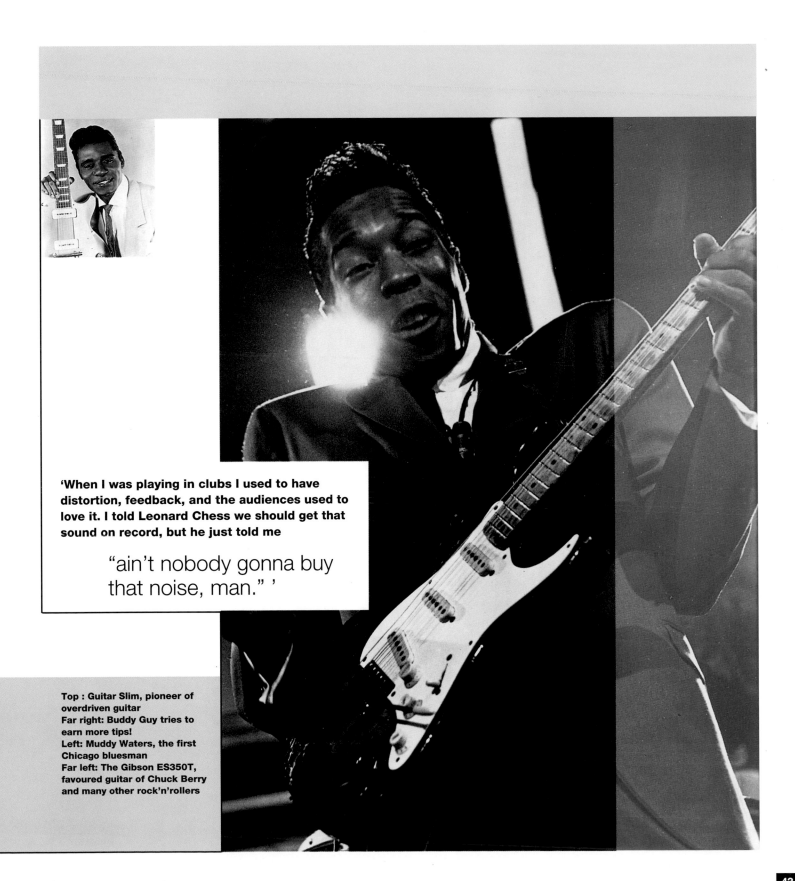

'When I was playing in clubs I used to have distortion, feedback, and the audiences used to love it. I told Leonard Chess we should get that sound on record, but he just told me

"ain't nobody gonna buy that noise, man." '

Top : Guitar Slim, pioneer of overdriven guitar
Far right: Buddy Guy tries to earn more tips!
Left: Muddy Waters, the first Chicago bluesman
Far left: The Gibson ES350T, favoured guitar of Chuck Berry and many other rock'n'rollers

History records Leo Fender as the inventor of the Broadcaster and Stratocaster, but generally omits his masterstroke: the electric bass.

While many inventors have laid claim to the concept of the electric guitar, Leo Fender's claim to the electric bass is beyond dispute. In one move he rendered the old fashioned upright bass – what he termed 'the doghouse' – obsolete, and changed forever the sound of popular music. Even more impressively, Fender's first rendition of the electric bass hardly differs from models still rolling off the production line 40 years later.

The original Precision, a simple slab of ash with a bolt-on maple neck, seems unprepossessing; original examples have acquired none of the mystique of a vintage Stratocaster or Les Paul. But this plain wooden creation paved the way for the Strat's radical double cutaway construction, and was far further removed from its acoustic antecedents than was the Les Paul from its cello-bodied forebears.

Fender Precision Bass | 1951

First electric bass guitar	
Designed 1950	
Commercially introduced 1951	
Revised 1957	
Production life 1951 to date	

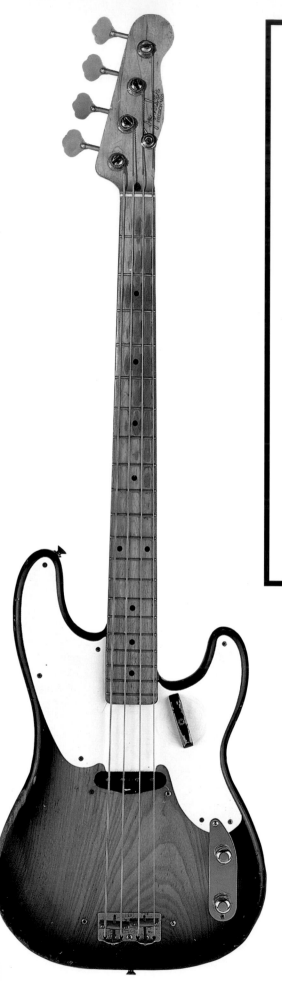

The concept of the Precision bass was simple. Leo Fender took the guitar-making principles that he'd established with the Telecaster, and applied these to the double bass, retaining the tuning but chopping 8" off the scale, dispensing with the body, and turning it on its side. The resulting electric bass was portable, easy to amplify, easy to play, and easy to mass produce. In its own way the instrument was just as revolutionary as the electric guitar; within ten years it had completely supplanted its stand-up predecessor.

While inventing the bass guitar, Leo Fender also established a precedent for the six-string electric. The body of the first Precision bass nowadays looks conventional – this makes it easy to overlook that this was the first electric guitar with two cutaways. At a time when many Gibson electric six-string guitars didn't even feature *one* cutaway, Fender spotted that by using two, and extending the upper horn over the neck, he could achieve better balance, and make his new instrument more playable. Fender's choice of a 34" scale length again seemed to have been plucked from nowhere, but the passage of time has shown his foresight.

In terms of construction, the Precision clearly shows its relationship to the Telecaster. The body is made of a single piece of ash with no contours, while the one-piece maple neck is simply attached by means of four screws. The bass features a simple single-coil pickup screwed down to the middle of the body, while a white phenolic plastic scratchplate protects the body and conceals the routing for the wiring. The electronics consist simply of one tone and one volume control on a Telecaster-style chromed plate. The bridge is one simple metal pressing; the strings pass over two saddles adjustable for height and intonation, before passing through the body and terminating at four ferrules at the back of the body.

The neck is, again, an enlarged version of the Telecaster's; it's made of one piece of maple, and the 20 frets are inserted directly into the neck, with the truss rod installed from the back, and adjusted at the body end. Leo called his bass the Precision because bassists could now fret notes accurately – a move that seems obvious now, but was unthought of in 1950. Fender's use of a 34" scale was a well-calculated one; it was small enough to

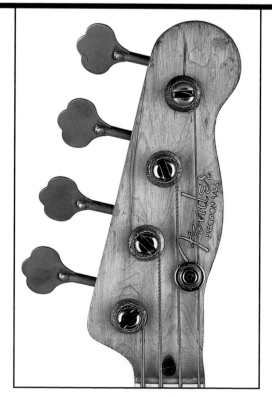

1

'I really like the roundness that the Precision has. I can get a real lot of top, and real lows, the mid-range – everything! The only change I've made is to de-wire the tone pot – when we used to play smaller places the fans'd lean forward and touch the controls! Now if I want to change the top end I look at my technician and point to my shoulder, with my thumb up or down – it's our little system.

If I want more bottom I pat myself on the arse.'

Steve Harris, Iron Maiden

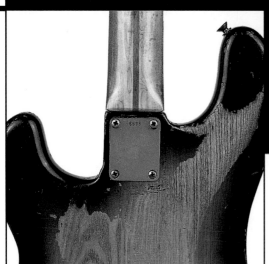

2

Main shot: The first Precision defined the shape, scale length and construction of the bass guitar
1. Tele-style headstock features enlarged guitar-style machineheads – far more efficient than the banjo style heads used by its later Gibson competitors
2. Compare this shot with the similar one of the Stratocaster on page 50; the Strat's much touted 'twin horns' made their debut on this instrument

enable guitarists to switch to the new instrument without much difficulty, but provided enough string tension to provide a strong, clean tone. The efficacy of this choice is perhaps best illustrated by the attempts of Fender's rivals to produce basses with smaller scales – they gave a thudding, tonally indistinct sound which won few fans.

Although solid body construction had profound implications for six-string guitars, the effect was perhaps even greater for the electric bass, particularly with the use of steel strings. The solid body increased sustain and emphasised higher harmonics, while the steel strings added brightness – together they gave a sound that was cleaner and more distinct than the instrument's upright cousin.

Playing an original 1955 example reveals just how much Fender got right; it has a clean punchy sound, with a woody depth which modern basses often lack. As on the Strat or Tele, the maple neck again reinforces the bass's presence; in a modern studio environment this example was ideally suited to DIing (direct injection) or amplifying, although electrical interference, due to the single-coil pickup, can be a real problem. The bass has just the one sound – and it's perfect. Modern basses might feature parametric equalization, active pickups and improved hardware, but still don't offer a significant improvement over the Precision in providing a well-defined but rounded bass end for the typical rock band.

Although Fender got so much right with the first version of this bass, its slab body was uncomfortable – this was rectified in 1954, to produce the version pictured here. By 1957 Fender had introduced the Precision bass with a larger headstock and, more importantly, a humbucking split pickup. This new model represented the state of the art for around 20 years – although some bassists felt the need for a second pickup, this was catered for by Fender's Jazz Bass, introduced in 1960.

Leo Fender's concept for the electric bass still dominates modern designs; it's a rare instrument that ignores the Precision's legacy. Even Ned Steinberger, whose bass designs are perhaps the furthest from Leo's original concepts, acknowledges that the original Precision was just as revolutionary as his own carbon graphite creation. And whereas the Steinberger still enjoys only cult appeal 10 years after its invention, the Precision had rendered its predecessor obsolete well within that timespan. No other instrument has ever looked so unassuming – or been quite so revolutionary.

The Fender Stratocaster is universally acknowledged as a design classic, even outside guitar-playing circles. This is largely due to the fact that it is the best selling guitar design ever, and over 40 years on remains in production, largely unchanged. Like Levi jeans or the Zippo lighter, it has achieved iconic status, yet the reason for this status has rarely been analysed. Even now, the crowning achievement of Leo Fender, working with George Fullerton and Freddie Tavares, tends to be taken for granted.

The Stratocaster, released in 1954, was conceived as an upmarket model that would sit alongside the basic slab-bodied Tele. The guitar's new features included the then-radical double cutaways, or 'horns', a revolutionary tremolo system, and a three pickup layout. But this was an instrument that was more than functional – it allowed for playing techniques which would only be developed years later by the likes of Jimi Hendrix or Jeff Beck. Furthermore, although the Strat was an expensive model to develop in terms of initial tooling, it was optimized for mass production, a fact that has allowed hundreds of copyists to plagiarize Fender's design, but has also, ironically, ensured the model's long-term survival.

Fender Stratocaster | 1954

| First double cutaway 3-pickup electric |
| The world's most copied guitar design |
| Designed 1951-1953 |
| Commercially introduced 1954 |
| Production life 1954 to date |

The Stratocaster's body, initially made from solid ash, was a straightforward development of the Telecaster. Leo had acknowledged that the Tele's shape looked unsophisticated, and responded with a sleek contoured body with two cutaways which is supremely comfortable, and whose aesthetic appeal remains timeless. Hailed as futuristic when it was launched, the passage of time has shown that the basic look of the Stratocaster transcends its era – its appeal today has nothing to do with nostalgia.

Crucially, it seems that the Stratocaster was the world's first double cutaway six-string electric guitar; this enabled better top fret access and improved the balance of the guitar, and has since become an industry standard.

The Stratocaster's one-piece maple neck was similar to that of the Telecaster, but with a new headstock design that was even more similar to that of the guitars that Paul Bigsby built for Merle Travis in the late '40s. Once again, the strings passed in a straight line from bridge to machine head, minimizing friction and aiding stable tuning. Fender retained the bolt-on neck that he had pioneered, primarily for ease of repair. This was, however, a need that rarely arose, again because of subtle but superlative design. Contemporary Gibson designs featured an angled neck and a back angled headstock; left on its back, a Gibson's weight would fall on this vulnerable point. The Fender design meant that weight was less likely to fall on the headstock, that the headstock was fundamentally stronger, and that the neck could be easily replaced if damage did occur.

The guitar's electronics were a major advance on its predecessor. The use of three pickups was marketing-led – its rivals had two pickups, therefore the Strat would have three. Yet whereas on most three pickup guitars the third

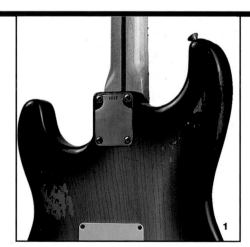

1

pickup is an encumbrance, on the Strat it enabled more sonic options, all the more so when guitarists discovered that the three-way switch, which selected each pickup individually, could be lodged between positions to give front and middle, or back and middle, combined. These pickups subtly interacted when used in pairs; strictly speaking they were not out of phase, but, because of the varying points at which they sensed the strings, gave a unique sound which has been demonstrated on countless records, from Buddy Guy, through Jeff Beck and Hendrix, to Mark Knopfler and Robert Cray.

The way in which the pickups were attached to the guitar was also unique – they were all mounted, complete with selector switch and tone and volume controls, on the large white phenolic scratchplate. This meant that the bulk of the wiring could be performed away from the guitar, a modular approach which simplified production, repair and modification.

The pickups themselves, all adjustable for height, differed from those of the Telecaster; all three were similar to each other in terms of

'Remember the first Strat I saw? I certainly do! I saw one hanging in the window of a music shop in Charing Cross Road. I was with a guy from the Deltones – we'd skipped off school and got the bus up to Victoria. From the top of the bus I said, **"I have seen the light!"** and went bowling down the stairs knocking the conductor out of the way, jumped off the bus and ran across the road. There was a sunburst Strat in the window and a blond Tele with an ebony fingerboard. I thought, **"This is it!"**

We went in and the guy in the shop asked if we were interested in buying it. We said, **"Y-y-y-yes!"** We were fourteen and he knew we didn't have the money but he let us play on it and it was like being on a cloud – we didn't come down for ages after.'

Jeff Beck (pictured with fellow Strat fan Buddy Guy)

Main shot: 1955 Fender Stratocaster
1. The double cutaway design, although featuring a bulky neck joint by contemporary standards, radically improved access to the top frets
2. The headstock was an elegant update of the Telecaster – it also bore a distinct resemblance to the headstock on Paul Bigsby's guitars
3. By 1959 the Strat had gained a dark, rosewood fingerboard, and custom colour finishes, such as the Olympic White of this 1962 example

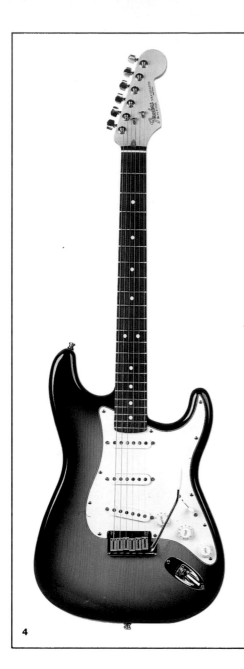

construction, with six staggered pole pieces, intended to even out volume discrepancies between the strings. The pickups themselves were perfectly matched for volume, their only real drawback being a tendency to pick up noise by virtue of their non-humbucking nature.

The Stratocaster sported three controls – a master volume, situated conveniently close to the bridge, and two tone controls, which operate on middle and neck pickups. Modern users have occasionally complained about the lack of a tone control on the brightest pickup; Fender, however, concentrated on achieving a brighter sound because of the poor treble response of contemporary amplifiers. The guitar's output jack socket was again unique; the actual socket was recessed in order to minimize damage to the jack plug if the guitar was dropped.

The Stratocaster's sound has become so ubiquitous as to almost render description redundant, but two properties are worth highlighting. Firstly, the versatility and practicality of the three pickup system. Secondly, the guitar's versatility in terms of amplification – the instrument has been used in every set up, from the DI method, where the instrument is directed straight into a recording desk to give no distortion whatsoever, through to its use with a bank of overdriven Marshall amplifiers.

Fender performed various modifications to the Stratocaster in its production life; some, such as the rosewood fingerboard introduced in 1959, have their adherents; others, such as the three bolt neck introduced in 1971, were introduced for valid reasons but are damned by virtue of their association with a period when Fender's production standards were falling.

Functionally, the Stratocaster is streets ahead of its peers, but it does have minor inconveniences that later derivatives have corrected. The aforementioned friction sources in the nut, string retainer, and tuning machines can be minimized by fitting a friction-reducing nut and string retainer, and locking machine heads – devices which were unavailable to Fender at the time of the guitar's development. Truss rod adjustment demands the inconvenience of removing the scratchplate. The guitar had a bulky neck joint; modern designs invariably chamfer or contour this feature for improved top fret access and comfort. Lastly, the pickups are susceptible to interference; pickup manufacturers have spent years trying to eliminate this problem while retaining the characteristic Strat sound, and 40 years on they've just about succeeded.

4

5

The Strat's tremolo bridge was, like so much of the guitar, rethought from first principles. (It should be pointed out that it is in fact a vibrato unit – tremolo refers to volume variation, whereas vibrato refers to pitch variation. This is a misnomer that Fender have standardized.)

Fender set themselves an ambitious target for the tremolo system – it should provide stable tuning, individual height and intonation adjustment for each string, and a limited amount of upbend, as well as downbend. In search of this target, Fender abandoned one early version, together with several thousand dollars' worth of tooling.

The unit, which acted as bridge, tailpiece, and vibrato system, was unlike anything that had appeared before. It worked on a fulcrum principle, pivoting around six screws which attached the unit to the guitar body at the front edge of the unit. String tension was counterbalanced by up to five springs, accessible via a plate at the back of the body. The strings passed through six adjustable pressed steel saddles and were anchored at the bottom of a heavy inertia block which itself contributed to the guitar's sound – many guitarists, such as Eric Clapton, who prefer not to use the tremolo, simply jam it in place with a wooden block rather than opting for a non tremolo model.

The Stratocaster tremolo has drawn grudging praise over the years, but the fact remains that with careful setup it is radically more effective than its contemporary alternatives. Leo's main aim was to reduce friction within the system, the major causes of which remain the pivot points, the nut, the string retainer, and the bridge saddles themselves. Modern tremolo systems, like that of the Paul Reed Smith guitar, minimize these friction sources while retaining the basic design of the system.

6

4. The current American Standard Stratocaster boasts only minor changes from early models, including a revised tremolo system and a flatter 9" fingerboard camber
5. This 1971 model features the wider headstock introduced in late 1965
6&7. 1973 model (front and back shown) boasts typical '70s features of ash body, shiny polyester finish, and three bolt neck joint with 'bullet' truss rod adjustment

7

Fender

1966-67 CATALOG

**Main shot: Leo Fender, who was rarely pictured away from his workshop
Above: Fender's publicity material stressed the company's modern image**

When Leo Fender died aged 82 in March 1991, many tributes were written praising the man who had started the Fender company In California back in the late '40s. After all, Fender had virtually invented the solid electric guitar. But Leo Fender's genius went beyond being a mere inventor. Of all his obituaries, perhaps the one which best summed up the essence of this great man's achievements made the point that 'Fender commercialized the existing idea of the solid-body electric guitar, applying simple and effective mass production techniques.'

This revolution in the making and marketing of guitars was the Fender company's masterstroke. Fender's early insistence on electric guitars that were relatively straightforward to put together and easy to mass produce had as much influence on the guitar-making industry as their original and magnificently simple instrument designs. As Dan Smith of the modern Fender company observes, 'Leo Fender was the Henry Ford of guitars.'

Some 40 years after Fender's introduction of the first commercially successful solid-bodied electric guitar, such conclusions might appear self-evident. But back at the dawn of the '50s, it must have been very different. There was no one to point the way, and precious few to offer the benefit of their experience.

In a few short years, Fender's original trio of Telecaster, Precision Bass and Stratocaster combined to establish in the minds of musicians and guitar-makers the idea of the solid-bodied electric guitar as a viable modern instrument. What is remarkable is that in these circumstances Fender got so much right, and almost always the first time. That trio of designs is still at the heart of the sustained success of the Fender Musical Instruments Corporation of today, which continues to turn out musical instruments with that famous logo. And virtually every maker of solid electric guitars has absorbed Fender influences, from the merest echo of a headstock shape to the blatant copying of complete guitars.

Leo Fender drifted into guitar-making. He opened a radio store in his native Fullerton, in the Los Angeles area in California, around 1940. As a result he met various local musicians who used to bring in amplifiers for repair. Leo got friendly with one in particular, Doc Kauffman, a violinist and lap-steel guitar player who had also worked with Californian guitar-maker Rickenbacker, and in 1945 Leo and Doc started the K&F company (Kauffman & Fender), making lap-steel electric guitars and small amplifiers.

There was a craze for lap-steel guitars in the States in the '30s and '40s.

and Mass Production

(Lap-steels differ from conventional 'Spanish' guitars in several significant ways, primarily in that they are played on the seated guitarist's lap, and the strings are played not by fretting but by holding a steel bar in the left hand and sliding it across the tops of the strings.) There was relatively little demand for electric 'Spanish' guitars at this time, so it was natural for K&F to build what was in demand.

And so in this low-key manner, as Kauffman built a small number of K&F instruments in inauspicious surroundings at the back of the radio store, Fender began to familiarize himself with pickups, amplifiers, and amplified guitars. Leo was ambitious, spotted the potential, and wanted to expand; Kauffman was less sure. So the two parted, and K&F ceased trading. Leo bought new premises nearby, formed the Fender Electric Instrument Co. in 1946, and continued to make lap-steels and amplifiers. He hired a few local women to help with assembly of the

re-named Fender products – and that's about as near as the small Fender company got to mass production in the late '40s. From various reports, it seems that they were nearer to bankruptcy than anything else at this stage.

There had clearly been a leap from this humble set-up to the massive production facilities for which the CBS conglomerate paid $13 million when they took over Fender in 1965. And somewhere along the line a decision was made to go into the electric 'Spanish' guitar market, in the shape of the virtually untried and untested solid-bodied variety.

One of the ex-Fender people I visited in California in 1992 to trace the story of the original Fender solid-bodied electric guitars was Forrest White, who was responsible for running production at Fender from 1954 to 1967. As we chatted about the past, seated in the library of the luxurious country club near Palm Springs in California where the 71 year-old White was living in splendid retirement, it became clear that he had created some profound and significant changes at Fender.

After speaking to my other interviewees, I concluded that White and sales boss Don Randall were the keys to Fender's original success in the '50s and '60s. Of course there were others, not least the workers who put the Fender instruments together on the shop floor in California, but White and Randall seemed to shine out. Leo Fender's much-touted 'genius' must have had a good deal to do with surrounding himself with clever, dedicated people.

White had joined the Fender company in spring 1954, and had come to Fender with a background in industrial engineering, primarily in the aircraft industry, and an interest in electric guitars. Some months before White's arrival, Leo had also hired lap-steel guitarist Freddie Tavares, primarily to collaborate on product designs and add a guitarist's point of view. This he certainly did, most spectacularly with the Stratocaster (1954) and Jazzmaster (1958).

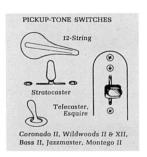

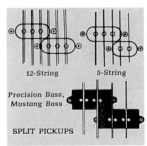

White remembered having lunch with Leo one day and being told about the problems the company was facing: they had no credit, having to pay cash for any materials purchased, and sometimes employees' cheques would bounce... particularly if Leo's wife was late in receiving her wages from her job at the local phone company. Tavares had told Leo that the only solution was to hire someone new with organizational skills. And in walked White.

'It just so happened that my timing was right,' White remembered with a grin. 'Leo says hey, I've been looking for someone for some time with your experience to help me with the management of the company. Would you be interested?'

White told Fender that he had a good job already, so he wasn't sure. He was asked to have a look around Fender's new buildings in Fullerton. 'Well, I looked. And it was a mess. There was no planning whatsoever – because Leo was not an engineer, he was an accountant. They had just moved into this place at South Raymond and he had four buildings there, 40 by 120. Things had just been set down any place. Now, I knew that in manufacturing you should have a flowchart so that things run smoothly from one operation to another. But everything was just so mixed up, I couldn't believe it.'

White eventually agreed to work for Leo so long as he was given a free hand to make changes. 'He gave me that free hand. When I stepped in, from that point on I ran the company.' Leo and Freddie stayed in design, said White, and Don Randall ran the sales side of Fender. 'When I started in May 1954 the production was very low, and there were about forty people working there.'

One of the most important changes White made, and one which eased Fender's path into mass production of musical instruments, was an incentive scheme for Fender's workers. 'I tied the incentive into quality control,' explained White.

'If you set an incentive plan and you don't tie it in to quality control, people turn the thing out and to heck with the quality. But it was set up so that each operator was an inspector. Let's say you were on an assembly line and you passed the product on to me. If it came over to me and I saw there was something wrong there that you hadn't done right I'd say hey, take it back, do it right... and only then will I accept it. That way every operator was an inspector. And that meant it was on their own time if it had to be re-worked. As long as they turned out good production that passed, they made good money, darned good money. But if someone loused up, hey, once the next guy accepted it, then it's his problem.'

White said that when he started at Fender in 1954 the manufacturing process for electric guitars was simple and effective. 'We bought our lumber in long lengths, 18 or 20 feet, ash or alder, whatever we were making – we'd make the Telecasters out of ash because of the [virtually transparent] blond finish. You'd cut the wood and glue them together so you'd have a block of wood that was the size of a guitar body.

'We had what we called router plates made out of quarter-inch steel in the shape of the guitar body, usually two different plates. You'd attach one to the bottom with a couple of screws, and you could drill on that side, where the neck plate and everything went. On the other side went the plate where the pickups and everything ran. So you always had a minimum of two plates, sometimes three depending on how sophisticated the instrument was – some might have more cut-outs and so on. So you'd screw those on, trace around them, band-saw the body roughly to shape, then you'd take off the excess on the router, and on to sanding.

'Then the necks. For ovalling you had a couple of holders swinging back and forth, and then there was a mandrel that had the holes cut out for the frets. Leo designed all of the tooling, or most of it, himself. It was very simple, but it was a case of having to walk before you ran. We didn't have any computerized routers and so on like they have now, where they can cut out half a dozen necks at a time. It was one at a time back then, and everything was simple. Crude, really, but it got the job done.

'It didn't change too much really. It was improved to a certain extent, but nothing like they have today. When I started in 1954 we were making about forty guitars a week, and when CBS bought the company in January 1965 we were making around fifteen hundred guitars a week.'

White was firmly of the opinion that CBS changed the company for the worse. 'They wanted production, and any way you could get it. So they weren't concerned about the quality. All they were looking at was the bottom line, profit, and they wanted a big profit. They were running it from New York, that's where those guys were located, and on your statement you'd better show the proper profit, or else they would get pretty upset with you,' he laughed.

Forrest White was certainly important in helping Fender change from a small specialist company to a large mass production unit capable of producing a huge range of instruments. At the end of 1954, the year White joined, their electric guitar list showed the new Stratocaster, the Telecaster, the Esquire, and the Precision Bass. When he left in 1967 CBS/Fender still had those four, plus the Jaguar, Jazzmaster, Mustang, Duo-Sonic, Musicmaster, Electric XII, Mustang Bass, Jazz Bass, Bass VI, and Bass V.

Fender had captured a huge segment of the market, selling their bright, modern-looking guitars with bright, modern-looking promotional material that contrasted favourably against the drab, traditional look of some of their competition. This was how Fender Sales head Don Randall and his team of salesmen transformed the company's fortunes, aggressively and creatively selling the 'fine electric

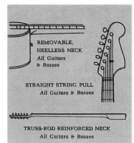

Main shot: gluing-in position markers, 1966
From left: the Jaguar, Jazzmaster and the
budget Musicmaster are today overlooked in
favour of the Strat, but all were popular
guitars; the Jazzmaster and Jaguar found
particular favour with US surf bands such as
The Beach Boys (above)

instruments' from Fullerton. As salesman Dale Hyatt, at Fender from 1946 to 1972, told me, 'You can make the finest guitar in the world, but if you don't sell the first one you're not going to get the chance to make another one.'

Of course, the competition was also busily catching on to the fact that young people were interested in buying large numbers of electric guitars, and Fender were by no means alone as the '60s progressed and the guitar sales boom peaked around 1972.

Guitar-players, collectors and dealers often refer to the purchase of Fender in 1965 by Columbia Broadcasting System Inc (CBS) as the point at which the company's creativity took a nosedive. The buy-out occurred because Leo Fender was worried about his health, so Don Randall was charged with arranging the sale of the Fender companies, which he completed by January 1965. Leo Fender stayed on as a theoretical 'consultant' for a few years, and gradually the rest of the old guard left CBS one by one. Certainly the quality of some Fender products deteriorated as the new CBS bosses pushed for maximum output at minimum cost, although there is no doubting the amount of money that CBS stuffed into Fender – such as the $1.3 million spent on a brand new factory, completed in 1966.

As an example of CBS's hardnosed attitude, consider their reaction to some of the waste stock that was building up in this new plant. They noticed that after models had been occasionally discontinued or dropped, bodies and necks and sundry hardware would be left over. Some makers might have recouped a little of their losses by selling the scrap wood as off-cuts or paper-mill pulp, perhaps, but CBS reaped an unexpected benefit from Fender guitars' bolt-together construction by mating together into 'new' guitars parts not originally intended for one another. This resulted in such malformed and short-lived models as the Custom and the Swinger, both released during 1969 to an unenthusiastic response.

During the '70s, one could say in retrospect that CBS took mass production to its logical conclusion. They focussed on Fender's most popular models – the Stratocaster and the Telecaster – and by 1980 this concentration was almost to the exclusion of new ideas and other models. CBS turned out the essential Fenders in

tens of thousands. Overall, as a result, quality slipped, no question about it. Dealers knew it, players knew it, CBS probably knew it too. And yet the common view among players and collectors that 'all '70s Fenders are rubbish' is exaggerated. It's just that more of the guitars that Fender made in the '70s were average than were good. And it often seems as if the good ones were produced in spite of rather than because of the company's activities.

The inevitable shake-up did not occur until the early '80s. A new management team was brought in, and they were determined to turn around Fender's flagging reputation and revitalize the company's dipping income. Ironically, the new blood was taken from the US arm of a Japanese company. The Japanese guitar-making industry had taken on the Americans, and the Orientals were winning. After a brief spurt of homegrown originality, the Japanese had insouciantly copied successful Western designs, primarily those of Fender and Gibson. At first these were cheap and relatively nasty efforts, but they got better. Much better. By the end of the '70s the Japanese were offering original designs and copies of reasonable quality, and had become serious competitors in a market that the United States had previously had more or less to itself.

The new management at Fender, primarily president Bill Schultz and director of marketing Dan Smith, decided that the only way to beat the Japanese was to hit them in their own market - and the only way to do that was to make guitars in Japan. So in 1982 the Fender Japan company was set up, licensed to build Fender guitars at the Fuji Gen-Gakki factory in Matsumoto, a plant which had already successfully provided export models of Ibanez-branded guitars. But the Fenders made there were initially just for Japanese domestic sale, designed to provide competition for the rising Japanese guitar-makers in their own (and most profitable) market. Fender HQ discovered that they could also sell these cheaper-to-produce Japanese-made Fenders elsewhere, and soon a range of Fender Japan models was being successfully exported to European and American markets, among others.

Despite the resulting boost in output and sales, CBS still had difficulty seeing this new light at the end of Fender's tunnel, and they decided to sell up. Eventually, in early 1985, almost exactly 20 years after they had acquired it, CBS sold Fender – excluding the factories – to an investor group headed by the existing management. The team quietly and slowly built up the company's reputation again. They used Japanese and Korean production to carry them through the short period they spent looking for a new American factory, which they eventually set up in Corona, California, by late 1985, and Fender's successful Custom Shop,

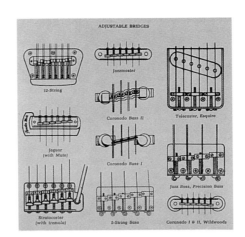

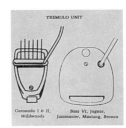

producing one-off custom orders and limited runs of specialist models, was set up close to the new factory in 1987. Fender continued to sell instruments produced in the Orient alongside American-made guitars, plus product from a new Fender factory in Ensenada, Mexico, which was established during 1990.

I visited the Corona factory in 1992, and found a busy mass production facility. From what I've been told about the old Fullerton factories in their heyday, there are parallels with the new plant – not least in the number of Hispanic women who work there. The basic processes are not far from what Forrest White would remember from the '50s and '60s. It's just that much has been automated, in line with most modern guitar making factories throughout the world. There are numerically (ie computer) controlled devices, such as that which puts a 'ledge' at one end of a fledgling neck and a 'groove' at the other, and many machines run suitable operations in duplicate, like one that shapes the curves on the back of eight necks at a time from a master. But there are still some jobs that have to be done by hand, such as the final blending of the neck shape, and much of the activity in the seven-booth paint shop, where facilities have been improved to give a cleaner environment for workers (and the surrounding country, too).

Thus the mass-produced Fender electric guitar lives on. What Forrest White and his co-workers achieved at Fender during the '50s and '60s was not just to do with the factory processes they applied to guitar-making. After all, even makers such as Gibson, traditionally noted for their hand-work and craft, still had guitars coming off production lines at their plants. Some form of factory-like assembly and organization is inevitable wherever more than a handful of guitars are produced. Fender simply exaggerated and exploited this aspect of guitar-making.

But the significant factor was that Fender's guitars themselves were among the first to be geared to mass production. There was no hand carving of guitar tops, no fancy inlays (not at first, at any rate), very little decoration, and, most important of all, the parts of the guitar simply bolted together.

In themselves these were not new ideas – very little of what Fender did was true innovation. But the company combined existing methods into a commercially viable whole, and applied what turned out to be apposite marketing schemes. They ensured that the fledgling rock'n'roll movement and its later offshoots like pop and rock were serviced with affordable guitars available in large numbers. Other companies succeeded in this way too, of course, but Fender got it going, and Fender were best at it. And they made some great musical instruments along the way, many of which helped shape the course of popular music, as everyone from Buddy Holly to Jimi Hendrix and Eric Clapton would attest.

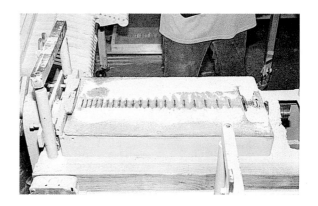

**Top and middle: Leo Fender designed a machine which would cut all the fret slots simultaneously
Bottom: Fender's main workshop, probably in the late '50s**

Gretsch guitars of the '50s rank as some of the most beautiful electrics ever made – and the company knew it. Where other manufacturers stressed playing features and star endorsements, the Fred Gretsch company boasted that their guitars were available in a wider range of colours than any of their competitors! Like American cars of the same era, Gretsches were colourful, sexy, and laden with gadgets, with an impracticality that is part of their charm. The Gretsch 6120, or Chet Atkins, ranks for many as the company's finest instrument, an amber and gold dream of a guitar that became an icon in the hands of Eddie Cochran or Duane Eddy. Fans of the instrument often comment that no two Gretsches ever sound alike; all the same, Gretsch guitars have a distinct warm but twangy sound, radically different from Gibsons or Fenders of the same era. At a time when modern guitar design appears more and more homogenized, these guitars are an ideal antidote.

Gretsch Chet Atkins 6120 | 1955

The definitive rockabilly guitar

Commercially introduced 1955

Revised 1962

Discontinued 1978

Original version reintroduced 1989

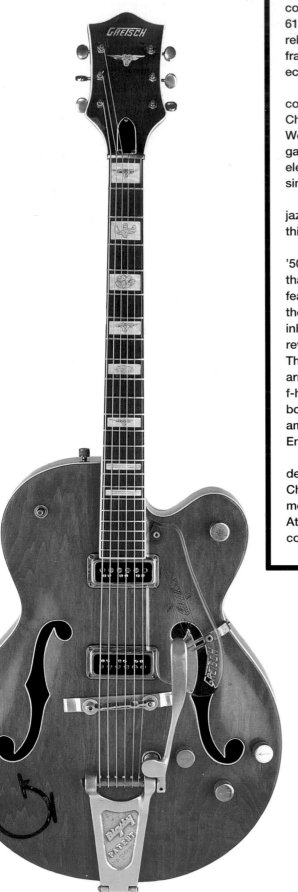

Most classic electric guitars have attained their status thanks to a combination of practicality and innovation. To be brutally frank, the Gretsch 6120 possesses neither of these attributes; Gretsches of this era tended to rely on gimmicks rather than innovative design, while vintage examples are fragile, and eccentric in many practical respects. But it is this very eccentricity which gives the guitar classic status.

Gretsch's electric guitar range was a reasonably conventional one until the company recruited chief designer Jimmy Webster and celebrated endorsee Chet Atkins in the early '50s. Both had strong ideas about guitar design; Webster was endlessly creative, with a strong bent towards '50s-style gadgetry, while Chet Atkins was intent on designing a simpler, sturdier electric guitar. Their collaboration resulted in a unique instrument which has since become regarded as the classic rockabilly guitar.

The Gretsch 6120 is a conventional shape, not dissimilar to the company's jazz-orientated Synchromatic models which preceded it. Yet in looks and feel this guitar seems far removed from its forebears.

Although rock'n'roll was starting to dominate the US charts in the mid '50s, the live music scene was mainly Country-orientated, and Gretsch used that imagery to the full in their new model. On its release in 1955, the 6120 featured a 'G' branded into the body and a longhorn motif on the headstock; the longhorn motif was repeated, together with cacti, on the fingerboard inlays. The pickguard was made of transparent perspex sprayed gold on the reverse; it bore Chet Atkins's signature on a rickety Wild West signpost motif. The metal control knobs carry Buck Rogers-style imprints of a G split by an arrow, and are seemingly scattered all over the place; three by the bottom f-hole, one by the cutaway, and a three-way pickup selector on the upper bout. The radio-age imagery is reinforced by the body colour – the shade of amber used is identical to the cast phenolic finish of '40s American Fada or Emerson radio sets.

Yet for all this apparent '50s overkill, a lot of thought had gone into the design. Most semi-acoustic guitars of the time featured wooden bridges; Chet Atkins specified a metal bridge to improve sustain, together with a metal nut – an innovative feature. Throughout the 6120's production life Atkins was to press for more solid construction of the guitar; Gretsch's concession to this was to provide extra bracing for the top, on to which the

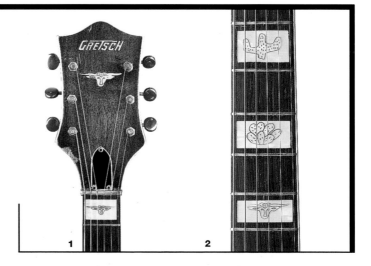

Main shot previous page: 6120 and the semi-solid body 6130 Roundup
Main shot this page: The Chet Atkins 6120 is the definitive rockabilly guitar
1. The guitar featured a metal nut for improved sustain
2. Classic model featured Western appointments such as these delectable cacti inlays!
3. This 1955 example features a 'fixed arm' Bigsby trem

'I had one of the first Les Paul guitars before I bought a Gretsch. It was a fine guitar, if you don't mind playing something with a neck that feels like a baseball bat.

'Then one day, I think it was 1956, I saw a Gretsch White Falcon in the local music store in Phoenix – it looked beautiful, but it cost six hundred dollars. But they had one more Gretsch, a red Chet Atkins. The neck on it was beautiful, much better than the Les Paul, so in the end I traded in the Gibson, and walked out with the Gretsch – I was paying $17 a month on top of that for a long time. That I remember! I've used that guitar on just about everything I've ever recorded. I've only played one other Gretsch with a neck that feels as nice as mine, and that's one that Ry Cooder bought which was made the same year as mine.

'As far as I'm concerned I've never played a guitar that sounded better. I don't take it on the road any more because the tuning keys are a bit delicate. I could put new keys on it but then it wouldn't be original. Also, if it was ever lost that would be the end of me.' *Duane Eddy*

pickups were mounted. Many of Atkins's ideas were later incorporated into the Gretsch Country Gentleman, released in 1959.

In comparison with its Fender and Gibson rivals, the 6120 was a fragile beast. A typical guitar weighs only 6.5lb, and the laminated, pressed back and top are thin (4mm) maple, with the sides slightly thicker at 5.5mm. The bridge, which was adjustable for overall height, but not for intonation or individual string height, was only attached to the body by string tension, and could easily be knocked out of position, sending the guitar out of tune. Similarly, the Bigsby tremolo – which would become an industry standard – demanded subtle usage in order to avoid tuning problems. The unit itself was reasonably effective, although the coil spring used could drop out with heavy upbends, but friction at the bridge and nut hindered return to correct pitch. In addition, on the original bridge design, the strings sat within grooves in the alloy bar; light gauge strings are free to move from side to side within the groove, to the extent of giving the guitar a remarkable sonic resemblance to a sitar. Some later models featured different bridge designs which allowed for individual intonation adjustment and could be used with any gauge strings.

Gretsch pickups have always been a major factor in their guitars distinctive sound. Earlier guitars featured single coil pickups made for Gretsch by DeArmond; in the mid '50s Chet Atkins introduced designer Ray Butts to the company; Butts had developed a humbucking pickup which Gretsch titled the Filtertron, and fitted to all their guitars by 1959.

Although the 6120 has its practical drawbacks, in use the sound more than compensates. Testing a 1956 model with DeArmond pickups revealed a surprisingly powerful output, with lots of top end, but a fatter sound than typical single coil pickups. The individual volume controls are useful – the neck pickup is louder than the bridge pickup – and overall the guitar exhibits a combination of powerful midrange and bright top end that's clearly distinct from the contemporary Fender or Gibson alternatives. Later Filtertron-equipped models had a unique sound too; these pickups are surprisingly quiet for humbuckers, but have a clear top end that humbucking pickups normally lack, due to the use of much smaller magnets and coils than Gibson-type humbuckers.

Gretsches have never masqueraded as purely functional instruments; all of their classic models, such as the Duo Jets or White Falcon have traded more on looks than ergonomics. Functionally, the guitar displays similar drawbacks to many '50s electrics – it is fragile, and tuning stability is hard to achieve with anything other than moderate tremolo usage. In addition, because of the skill required in assembling these guitars, Gretsches exhibit a wide quality range – in fact, the reissued models made from 1989 are probably superior in workmanship (if not in character) to their forebears.

For all these reasons, it's not surprising that Gretsch guitars are regarded more as covetable collector's pieces than as major influences on the course of guitar design. For all that, they are undeniably great guitars, and most importantly of all boast a sound which is just not attainable with any other design.

Gretsch Chet Atkins 6120 | 1955

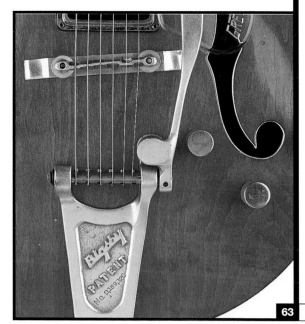

The reputation of the Gibson guitar company was primarily built on its excellent jazz-orientated hollow body electrics. The company's Les Paul guitar was a radical, but reluctant, step forward. With 1958's ES335 Gibson showed they could fuse the two traditions, delivering one of the most versatile guitars ever made.

The ES335 was a unique synthesis of solid and hollow body electric guitar, equally at home in sophisticated jazz or high volume rock'n'roll settings. For this reason it would prove Gibson's most enduring classic, its slim body, symmetrical double cutaways and central sustain block defining forever the shape and construction of the 'semi-acoustic' guitar. As one of Gibson's best-selling professional instruments, the 335 has never acquired the rarity value – or cachet – of the company's Les Paul Standard, but perhaps the ultimate tribute to this classic instrument came from Fender, who'd done so much to launch Gibson into the solid electric guitar business. They launched their own derivative, the Starcaster, in 1976.

Gibson ES335 | 1958

First 'semi-acoustic' guitar

Designed 1957

Commercially introduced 1958

Production life 1958 to date

'I knew I liked the 335 from the first time I played one. The first one I had was a brown sunburst, and **the main thing about that guitar was that the neck was so thin, and the body was so shallow so it was comfortable to play,** even back then when I was somewhat slimmer than I am now. Now I use a 355, the one with what I call the magic switch – I have it in the centre, which means both pickups are working, but I control each of them separately without even touching the volume switch – then when I'm playing live I adjust the volumes for both pickups constantly. A few years back I approached Gibson to develop the Lucille model, but I don't know if they're still producing it now – I haven't heard from them for a few years.' *B.B. King*

Throughout the '50s, Gibson jazz guitars had been moving to a 'thinline' design with models such as the ES350T and ES225T – these were more manageable, and slightly less prone to feedback than their deep bodied forebears. Over the same period the company had introduced the Les Paul, a radical step which had disturbed many conservative guitarists. Company president Ted McCarty had the idea of building a thinline jazz model which incorporated a solid bar down the middle, with the aim of obtaining the depth of sound of a solid body, and the sustain of a hollow body, together with a manageable weight. Gibson's design staff responded with a guitar which masterfully combined those aims.

The ES335T, as it was known on its introduction in 1958, looked completely unlike any 'jazz' guitar that had gone before. The hardware was all new – it appeared the same year on the Les Paul – and the guitar boasted two cutaways, in an elegant design that offered unparalleled access to the top of the guitar neck. Even those who didn't understand the implications of its radical construction thought it looked striking.

The key feature of the guitar was its maple sustain block, which ran through the middle of the guitar from the strap button at the base of the body, right through to the glued neck joint. Glued-in spruce strips join the block to the contoured maple top and back of the guitar. Pickups, bridge and tailpiece are attached directly to this middle section, making this part of the body act like a conventional solid body electric. The remainder of the body is free to resonate, and the two acoustic side chambers with unbound f-holes give more depth, and a much woodier sound than, say, a Les Paul.

The guitar's body was constructed fairly conventionally, from a pressed 5mm thick four-ply maple laminate. Yet the symmetrical cutaway bouts are a unique shape that's often referred to as 'Mickey Mouse ears' – for obvious reasons! These cutaways, together with a very slim neck-to-body join, offered top fret access that was far superior to any arch-top, as well as Fender's solid-bodied Stratocaster. This superlative access was complemented by a classic Gibson neck; made from mahogany with a rosewood fingerboard, the flat fingerboard and wide frets are ideal for jazz and blues players.

The control layout and hardware on the guitar was the epitome of simplicity. Two of Seth Lover's new humbucking pickups were selected by a three-way switch, with individual tone and volume controls for each pickup. The guitar also used Ted McCarty's recent ABR-1 tune-o-matic bridge. This unit was unique in an 'arch-top' context for several reasons; firstly it was fully adjustable for intonation, and height could be adjusted by two thumbwheels.

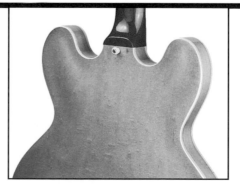

1

Secondly, it was all-metal, and mounted directly into the body, giving a more distinct edge to the tone. The stud tailpiece which anchored the strings was another departure from the arch-top convention of a trapeze tailpiece, and gave better sustain thanks to the sharper break angle over the bridge. Gibson in fact reverted to a standard trapeze tailpiece later in the guitar's life, and these models are generally regarding as having worse sustain than the original arrangement.

The 335's headstock is a typical Gibson design, which the company now refers to as an SP1. It's restrained and traditional, and tilts back, like the Les Paul, at an angle of 17°. This back angle, as detailed in the Les Paul entry, makes the headstock vulnerable to damage, but has a substantial effect on the guitar's sound. Increasing this angle increases string tension, which gives a firmer feel and more attack to the note. A shallower neck angle is easier to produce and less susceptible to damage, but gives a vaguer tone. Although '70s models departed from this standard, Gibson now regard the 17° angle as the perfect compromise – imitators have departed from this value at their peril!

2

Testing a 1960 model, the guitar's virtues are readily apparent. The bridge pickup has a thick, full and strident tone with a long sustain, while the neck pickup is dark and bluesy. Although neck profiles of 335s have varied over the years, early models are beautifully slim and wide, and together with the guitar's light weight (around 7.5lb) make the ES335 one of the most comfortable and playable guitars of its era.

For a guitar that possesses many of the attributes of fragile arch-tops, the ES335 is remarkably practical – indeed, while the Les Paul was discontinued in 1960, the ES335 has remained in uninterrupted production since its launch. Tuning on non-Bigsby models is stable, the guitar is resistant to electrical interference, and its basic design seems to have left little room for improvement. Ironically, the durability and longevity of the guitar means that values of late '50s models are around a third of that of comparable era Les Pauls.

Main shot: The ES335 was an elegant blend of hollow-bodied and solid-bodied styling
1. This double cutaway design was later copied by many companies including Gretsch, Harmony and Hofner
2. Typical Gibson hardware of humbucking pickups and tune-o-matic bridge – simple and efficient

The '60s:

The British

'The day the music died' was how Don McLean summed up a generation's reaction to Buddy Holly's plane crash in the song 'American Pie'. Holly was a popular rock'n'roll star who had yet to reach his true potential; his death in 1959 robbed the movement of one of its most promising musicians. With Elvis seeming to desert rock'n'roll in favour of a more mainstream career, Chuck Berry sentenced to a three-year jail sentence for an 'immorality offence' and Bill Haley's Comets distinctly burnt out, rock'n'roll had lost the momentum of the late '50s.

But while a new generation of anodyne pap was clogging the charts in the USA, something was stirring across the Atlantic. In Britain a skiffle revival led by Lonnie Donegan utilized the basic materials that were available in post-war Britain – acoustic guitar, washboards, kazoos and tea-chest bass – to provide what would be a stepping stone between US rock'n'roll and British beat music. But perhaps the supreme symbolic moment of that period was the arrival of the first 'proper' electric guitar in the country. Hank Marvin, guitarist with Cliff Richard and The Shadows, had persevered with a primitive Japanese-made Antoria electric. Now the band were making some real money, Cliff decided his guitarist should have the real thing.

'We had a brochure sent over,' recalls Marvin, 'and pored over it. We knew James Burton used a Fender, and assumed it would be the top line model. So we ordered the most expensive Strat there was, with bird's eye maple neck, tremolo arm, and gold-plated parts. Then we found out later on that James Burton was using a battered old Telecaster!

'It's difficult to describe what it was like seeing that instrument for the first time. It's pretty old hat now, because everybody's seen so many, but at the time it was like seeing an instrument from another planet, it just didn't look like a guitar!'

It's hardly an exaggeration to say that it was Marvin's Strat and a collection of blues records that inspired the British beat boom. It was after seeing Marvin play his shiny new Fender that guitarists from Jeff Beck and Richard Thompson to Brian May decided that they had to buy an electric guitar. Meanwhile, significant musical meetings were taking place all over the country.

'It must have been around 1958 that I heard John Lee Hooker, plus Muddy Waters and all those Chicago blues guys,' recalls Keith Richards. 'I would have been about fifteen or sixteen, I was at art school and records were passing around between aspiring guitar players and bluesmen – bored sixteen-year-old kids. The fact we were searching out these records kept us together.'

Are Coming!

The same story was being repeated in Manchester, where John Mayall was listening to his father's blues records; in Surrey, where future members of the Yardbirds, Pretty Things and Rolling Stones built up an incestuous blues scene; in Newcastle, where a spotty kid called Eric Burdon decided to join the Alan Price Combo, soon to be known as The Animals; and in Liverpool, where a band called The Beatles was living off a diet of Chuck Berry, Buddy Holly and Little Richard records. Serving their musical apprenticeship playing the seedy red-light district of Hamburg, The Beatles learnt a wide range of material including rock'n'roll covers, R&B songs and popular standards. Performing such a wide range of material gave them a vast musical vocabulary to draw upon when the Lennon–McCartney partnership started writing original material in earnest. The Beatles' line-up as a small, self-contained four-piece who began to write their own material was the first of its kind, inspiring many other musicians to pick up electric guitars and form bands – before The Beatles, singers had relied on back-up musicians and on songwriters to supply the material.

The actual instrumentation The Beatles used was similar to that of their American idols; Paul McCartney played a German-made Hofner violin bass, John Lennon a Rickenbacker 325 and George Harrison played a black Gretsch Duo Jet, bought second-hand from an American sailor. Lennon apparently bought his Rickenbacker having seen the jazz guitarist Toots Thielemans playing a Rickenbacker in Hamburg – a fortuitous moment for the American company. Many other Mersey-based bands followed in The Beatles' wake, although few approached their songwriting skills or sheer musical innovation. By February 1964, the Beatles had received the ultimate accolade of a Number One single in the US – the homeland of rock'n'roll – but despite the frenzy of continuous promotion and touring the band still found time to push the limits of contemporary music. Songs like 'Ticket To Ride' and 'Paperback Writer' combined heavy riffs with what at the time were radical song constructions – and were still naturally commercial. As Harrison remembers: 'I read somewhere that after the Beatles appeared on the Ed Sullivan Show Gretsch sold 20,000 guitars a week or something like that. I mean, we should have had shares in Fender, Vox, Gretsch and everything!'

Main shot: In a decade which was otherwise dominated by British guitarists, Jimi Hendrix was a revelation
Top right: Keith Richards, photographed in November 1964, was the first notable '60s exponent of the Les Paul Standard
Bottom left: Paul McCartney and Hofner violin bass

The Beatles also effectively rejuvenated the American music scene, inspiring bands like The Byrds, and even the already-established Beach Boys. In a further example of musical crossbreeding, Bob Dylan was inspired to go electric by The Animals' version of 'House Of The Rising Sun' – ironically, The Animals' arrangement of this tune had been influenced by Dylan's own rendition of it on his debut album. For a few short years British and American bands were united by common admiration, and rivalry. By 1966, the Beatles, however, had outstretched the musical equipment of the day and retired from touring, mainly because they couldn't make themselves heard in front of large audiences of screaming fans – PA technology was still very basic.

British R&B | As The Beatles were inspiring the Merseybeat sound in Liverpool, in London The Rolling Stones were heading an altogether rawer R&B boom. Originally led by Brian Jones, the band's sound developed from a straightforward, spirited imitation of Chicago blues, to innovative self-written material as Mick Jagger and Keith Richards took the helm. Richards experimented with several guitars in the '60s, including Guilds, Gretsches and Epiphones, but was also the first famous British guitarist to use a Gibson Les Paul – he was using one by 1964. Richards was also one of the first guitarists to use a fuzz box on 1965's '(I Can't Get No) Satisfaction'. That song provoked an early Jagger–Richards argument – Richards thought his own composition was a simplistic gimmick and didn't want to release it as a single.

Over the years Richards' style became more and more distinctive; following Brian Jones's death in 1969 he learned a new tuning, open G, from Ry Cooder, who was drafted in as a studio guitarist. Richard found that this new tuning, with the bottom string removed, was perfect for his minimal rhythm style; or, as he puts it, 'all you need is five strings, three fingers, and one asshole.'

The Yardbirds moved in similar circles to the Stones, and when the Stones became too big for their residence at Richmond's Crawdaddy Club, The Yardbirds approached the Crawdaddy's manager, Giorgio Gomelsky, offering to replace them. Gomelsky jumped at the chance, and also took on the band's managership – an opportunity he'd let slip past him with the Stones.

The Yardbirds' lead guitarist, Top Topham, was 15 when his band got their break. Unfortunately his parents wouldn't stand for the teenager working late every night, so the job went to one Eric Clapton who, like Topham, attended Kingston Art School. Clapton was a competent guitarist but was soon to become the prototype for a new species – the guitar hero.

One of the band's first major engagements was backing up Chicago bluesman Sonny Boy Williamson in December 1963. Williamson was delighted at the attention he received, but on his return to America is said to have told another aspiring white blues guitarist, Robbie Robertson, 'Those English guys want to play the blues so bad. And they play it so bad!' Clapton became increasingly frustrated by The Yardbirds' attempts to achieve mainstream success, and left the band after recording the single 'For Your Love', convinced he could not be replaced. Within a matter of weeks The Yardbirds recruited Jeff Beck from The Tridents; with Beck the band would get progressively heavier, all the more so when new member Jimmy Page moved over from bass to second lead guitar.

Clapton, meanwhile, was recruited to John Mayall's Bluesbreakers, where according to the band's producer Mike Vernon he showed a whole new side to his guitar-playing. 'I think it was a shock to people who'd only seen him play with the Yardbirds – he'd stepped into different shoes altogether.' When he joined The Bluesbreakers Clapton became the first guitarist to exploit fully the tonal possibilities of a Les Paul played through a cranked-up Marshall amp. According to rock legend, the engineer on the 1966 *Blues Breakers* album, Gus Dudgeon, repeatedly asked Clapton to 'turn it down!' because – heaven forbid! – the sound from Clapton's 1962 model 45W 2 x12" Marshall combo was distorting.

Jimmy Page, then a session musician who frequently worked on sessions with the producer Shel Talmy, was friends with Clapton and Beck, and although he'd already experimented with fuzzbox distortion, credits Clapton's discovery of the Marshall amplifier as a pivotal moment.

'Eric was the first one to evolve the sound with the Gibson and Marshall amps – he should have total credit for that. I remember when we did 'I'm Your Witchdoctor' [in June 1965], he had all that sound down, and the engineer, who was co-operating up to that point (I was producing) but was used to orchestras and big bands, suddenly turned off the machine and said, "This guitarist is unrecordable!" The guy just couldn't believe someone was getting that kind of a sound from a guitar on purpose. Feedback, tremolo, he'd never heard anything like it.

'I don't know who was the first guitarist [to use feedback], I really don't. Townshend, of course, made it a big feature of his scene, because he couldn't play single notes. Beck used it. I used it as much as I could.'

Clapton left Mayall's band in 1966 after the one, hugely influential album, *Blues Breakers*. Mayall was quite sanguine about Clapton's departure – 'It's quite easy replacing a lead guitarist. It's if you lose a bassist that you're in trouble.' But then he could afford to be – he had another startling guitarist waiting in the wings. Peter Green had previously deputized for Clapton when the guitarist had

'all you need is **five strings, three fingers, and one asshole.'**

Main shot: By 1968 Keith Richards had elevated rhythm guitar to an art form
Inset: Jimmy Page (second from left) joined The Yardbirds as bassist, but soon switched to guitar
Opposite: Yardbirds lineup with Eric Clapton

'Eric was the first one to evolve the sound with the Gibson and Marshall amps. I remember when I recorded with him the engineer turned off the machine and said

"this is unrecordable!"

'The guy just couldn't believe someone was getting that kind of a sound from a guitar on purpose.'

disappeared without warning for a holiday in Greece, and although in some respects Green was influenced by his predecessor, he was a more than adequate replacement. Like Clapton, Green also recorded only one album with Mayall, then left to form Fleetwood Mac. In his turn Green was replaced by the shy but capable Mick Taylor, who would later replace Brian Jones in The Rolling Stones.

Fleetwood Mac's debut album was released in 1968. Ranking alongside the *Blues Breakers* LP as one of the most influential albums of the British blues boom, it was followed by a string of successful singles showing that Green's talent was not limited to that idiom. Green's main guitar was the 1959 Les Paul used on Fleetwood Mac's 'Need Your Love So Bad'. Legend has it that Green's unique tone came from an out-of-phase pickup arrangement when the guitarist took the guitar apart to clean it, then accidentally re-fitted one pickup the wrong way round. The guitar is now owned by Gary Moore, who comments, 'Other people have tried to get that sound on other Les Pauls by reversing the bass pickup but it doesn't sound the same – that guitar definitely has its own characteristic sound.' No doubt the way Green played had something to do with it as well.

After leaving the Bluesbreakers, Clapton formed Cream in 1966, also creating the concept of the 'supergroup'. Cream created the 'power trio' format, legitimizing lengthy on-stage jamming and loud volume – by the time of Cream's first album in 1966, Clapton was using 100 Watt Marshalls instead of the 45 Watt combo he had used with Mayall, with a corresponding change in tone. Cream bassist and singer Jack Bruce recalled the origins of the extensive improvisation: 'It all started in our first US tour in 1967. I remember the Fillmore in particular. When we arrived we were still doing the five minute pop song – verse chorus, verse chorus. When we got there the audience was on the dark side of the moon, shouting "just play, man, just play". But having to do that every night was what broke us up – they worked us to the point of death.'

No one knows if the 'Clapton is God' graffiti that was sprayed around the walls of London was real or apocryphal. But even if Clapton had acquired God-like status by the mid '60s, he was to be shaken to the core by a guitarist who arrived in London in September 1966.

Left: Cream, pictured in 1967: Jack Bruce, Eric Clapton (centre) and Ginger Baker pioneered the 'power trio' format
Right: Fleetwood Mac's Peter Green was one of the decade's most notable exponents of the Les Paul. His guitar, now owned by Gary Moore, is pictured far right

The Jimi Hendrix Experience

Jimi Hendrix was a spectacular showman from the T-Bone Walker and Little Richard Schools of Cool Moves but, more than that, his pioneering guitar-playing showed just how much is possible with the electric guitar. Brought to London by his manager, ex-Animal Chas Chandler, Hendrix was already an extrovert guitarist before he discovered the possibilities which opened up by combining his favoured Fender Strat with British Marshall amplifiers. The Jimi Hendrix Experience's debut album *Are You Experienced* stands as perhaps the most important electric guitar album to this day. Using recent innovations such as controlled feedback and backwards guitar in imaginative but highly musical structures, Hendrix held his music together with his solid blues grounding, influencing all guitarists who heard it. Always experimenting with equipment and ways to create new sounds or to capture the sounds he heard in his head, as often as not Hendrix was creating his sound despite his equipment rather than because of it. Hendrix was the first to discover the ultimate potential of the Fender Strat – and the first to discover its limitations. His excessive use of the tremolo arm caused the guitar to go out of tune – a problem only relatively recently rectified with the locking tremolo.

While the popular press would delight in promoting the 'Wild Man of Rock' aspect, Hendrix's music was just as much tender and lyrical as it was aggressive and thrusting. Although the Strat had three pickups and a corresponding three-way selector switch Hendrix used Buddy Guy's technique of lodging the switch midway between these positions to obtain two additional tones.

The combination of bass and middle pickup through a clean amp gives a particularly attractive chiming and hollow tone which Hendrix used extensively on the second JHE album *Axis: Bold as Love* in 1967 for tracks such as 'Little Wing', 'Castles Made of Sand' and 'One Rainy Wish'. This combined 'chord/melody' style of playing was not an entirely new technique, but Hendrix took it further, creating a new genre of playing in which the melody and chords are played simultaneously by fingering chord fragments and playing other notes 'on top'. This technique would later be used by guitarists as diverse as Steve Vai and Prince. Although Hendrix is often associated with distorted tones, it should be noted that on many of these songs Hendrix connected his Strat directly to the mixing console, in order to capture a pure, undistorted sound.

Although Hendrix is famous for sacrificing his guitar at Monterey in 1967, he wasn't the only one to indulge in 'destruction as art'. The Who, Jeff Beck and The Velvet Underground had all similarly used feedback, noise or instrument trashing as part of their performance. The Velvet Underground were pioneers of much of what later became regarded as the British punk movement, delighting in the possibilities of feedback unleashed by guitarist Sterling Morrison's Gretsch Country Gentleman, combined with a cranked-up Vox amplifier. Morrison still recalls that 'when we recorded our second album the engineer told us we had to turn down, that the meters were all into the red. We couldn't, it was an integral part of the sound we were after. Now, of course, I listen to that album and it's all noise!' Founder Velvets member John Cale would go on to produce the first album by seminal punks Iggy Pop and The Stooges in 1969.

Metal Gurus

The same British blues scene that dominated much of the '60s was also to result in a band which would dominate much of the '70s. Jimmy Page had formed Led Zeppelin in 1968, originally to fulfil contractual obligations incurred by his previous group, The Yardbirds. Although it wasn't until the '70s that the full range of Page's talents became apparent, *Led Zeppelin I*, released in 1969, offers some hints. A largely blues rock album powered by the thunderous drumming of John Bonham, Page's acoustic guitar influences of Bert Jansch and Davey Graham are apparent on the acoustic 'Black Mountain Side'. The follow-up album, Led Zeppelin II, also released in 1969, is held by some to be the first 'heavy metal' album. Page achieved the often-imitated-but-never-equalled tone on the opening track 'Whole Lotta Love' using a combination of his 1959 Les Paul Standard through a heavily distorted amp miked at a distance. In musical terms the band offered a cranked-up version of Willie Dixon's blues songwriting – indeed, the band would later settle out of court for having 'borrowed' one of Dixon's riffs for that very song.

But although Led Zeppelin, and many other British bands, had started from the blues, by the end of the decade they had altered the music almost beyond recognition. By the time it reached its zenith, Chicago blues was regarded as outdated by the very audiences it was trying to reach. In 1970, when popular music had changed the outlook of a generation and apparently stopped a war in Vietnam, it looked as if the electric guitarist was the most potent creature on the planet.

Most significant electric guitars took years to be recognized as classics. The Rickenbacker 360-12 achieved immortality by the time the second instrument had come off the production line. The only commercially significant 12-string electric, the 360-12 was instantly taken up by the likes of The Beatles, The Byrds and The Beach Boys, and provided the most distinctive electric guitar sounds of the mid '60s.

The 360-12 combines practicality and eccentricity in equal measures. The headstock design is masterful in its simplicity, while the body was a complex mix of solid and semi which meant this guitar was difficult to build – and even more difficult to copy. Both Gibson and Fender attempted to match the success of Rickenbacker's 12-string; but like all classic models the 360-12's sound became regarded as definitive and saw off its competitors.

As a practical guitar design the 360 seems wilfully obscure – practically no element has any similarity to other guitars. Even the paint finish is a secret extra thin formula while the hardware is unique, from the chunky cast R tailpiece, through the rubber grommets that isolate the pickups from the solid top, to the flatwound strings which according to Who guitarist Pete Townshend are an integral part of the Rickenbacker sound. Yet Rickenbacker also boasted design elements, like efficient double cutaways for easy top fret access, that were years ahead of the competition.

Rickenbacker 360-12 | 1964

First commercially significant electric 12-string
Designed 1963
Commercially introduced 1964
Revised 1965
Production life 1964 to date

1

The Rickenbacker company were pioneers of the electric guitar, but assumed a fairly low profile at the start of the '60s; Gibson, Fender and Gretsch all enjoyed greater visibility throughout the rock'n'roll era. That would change with the advent of The Beatles.

John Lennon had acquired a Rickenbacker 325 in Hamburg in 1960, while George Harrison bought a 425 some time later. Even before The Beatles enjoyed their first US hit, Rickenbacker president F.R. Hall realized the value of his unofficial endorsees as a string of English wholesalers contacted Rickenbacker seeking UK distribution rights. By the time of The Beatles' first visit to America in February '64, Hall was well prepared, and presented Harrison with a 360-12. Harrison sang the guitar's praises during the course of a radio interview for a Minneapolis radio station; the station bought the guitar for him as a gift.

The origins of the 360 lay in the 'Capri' series of guitars designed by Rickenbacker's Roger Rossmeisl in the late '50s. Rather than using the separate top and sides of a conventional semi-acoustic, Rossmeisl machined out the soundchamber

from the back of a solid lump (usually two pieces, centre-joined) of maple, with a separate two-piece back. The Capri guitars featured two generous cutaways, while a neck joint set well into the body (up to the bridge pickup) gave a very stiff construction. Rickenbacker were experimenting with neck through body construction by 1956, and in their pursuit of easy access to the top frets were well in advance of Gibson or Fender.

The 360-12 was first developed at the instigation of F.R. Hall at the end of

1963. It utilized the typical Capri construction techniques, but featured 12 strings. The second example made featured 'reverse' stringing – when strumming downwards the bass octaves sound first. This enabled easier fretting of all the strings and gave a distinctive sound which has since become identified with Rickenbackers, for it was this 'reverse strung' example that Hall presented to Harrison. The Byrds' Roger McGuinn was inspired to buy a 360-12 after seeing Harrison use one in the film *A Hard Day's Night,* and the guitar became an integral part of the newly-emerging folk rock movement, regarded as the definitive electric 12-string despite the prior existence of 12-string models by Stratosphere, Gibson and Danelectro.

Playing a 1966 example, it's remarkable how the 360-12 has a distinctive '60s ambience, and yet feels surprisingly contemporary. The quality of construction is exemplary (Rickenbacker never suffered the quality control problems experienced by Gibson and Fender in the late '60s). The three-piece laminate neck is very slim, aided by Rickenbacker's proprietary dual truss rods, although the highly lacquered African rosewood fretboard doesn't feel 'worn in', even after more than 25 years. The headstock design is economical and enables perfect balance, although restringing the octave strings is extremely fiddly. Control layout is straightforward, with tone and volume for each pickup and a small 'balance' control. The guitar's sustain is impressive, although like most Rickenbackers the 360 does not suit a cranked up distorted sound; instead it's best used with a moderately loud but clean valve amp, for that instantly recognizable 'chiming' sound.

Although eccentric, the 360 boasts impressive ergonomics: the neck is comfortable despite the cramped spacing while sustain and tuning stability are good. That distinctiveness explains why the instrument has never become ubiquitous, but as modern trends turn in favour of more distinctive sounds, the Rickenbacker still seems curiously contemporary.

2

Main shot: The model featured is the 1966 360-12 with contoured top
1. Headstock design is brilliantly compact
2. Pickups are isolated from body by rubber grommets

'You can hear George play his Rickenbacker 12-string in the actual song A Hard Day's Night, the solo. After I saw the film **I went right out and bought one.** We recorded that guitar through two compressors which gave amazing compression and sustain. And that was it, that jingle jangle sound, as simple as that.'

Roger McGuinn *The Byrds*

In the history of the electric guitar, some instruments have been classic since their inception; others have had greatness thrust upon them. Perhaps the classic example of the latter species is the Hofner violin bass. First produced in 1956, this modest, low-priced instrument was a steady seller in its native German market, both to local musicians, and, from the late '50s, touring British bands. In early 1961, Paul McCartney, who'd recently taken up bass with The Beatles, bought one of these budget basses in Hamburg for DM350.

The Hofner violin bass is largely hand made in a factory that specialized in violins, violas and double basses. In production to this day, the guitar is fragile, temperamental, primitive – and totally ravishing, for its sound has become part of the pop music psyche, providing the bedrock for Beatles' songs from 'Love Me Do' to 'The Ballad Of John and Yoko'. It is a salutary reminder that guitars don't have to be expensive or superbly functional in order to become classics.

Hofner Violin Bass 1956

Budget-priced European bass

Designed 1955-1956

Commercially introduced 1956

Revised 1964

Production life: 1956 to date

The Hofner Musical Instrument company was originally one of Germany's many violin factories, founded by Karl Hofner in 1887 and making violins under their own name as well as supplying bodies to other violin factories. Over the succeeding years Hofner's sons, Josef and Walter, joined the family firm. When the company's original factory at Schönbach was nationalized after the Second World War, Walter was instrumental in setting up a new operation in Bubenreuth in 1951, and recognized that arch-top guitars constituted an area ripe for expansion. The company produced their first electrics around 1953, and when Walter Hofner decided to produce an electric bass guitar three years later, it was perhaps no surprise, given the company's violin-making background, that he should give it a traditional violin outline.

The Gibson company had produced a violin-shaped bass in 1953, a couple of years after Leo Fender had premiered the Precision bass. Gibson's instrument was a commercial failure, with only a few hundred sold in its five-year life span. No examples are known to have been exported to Europe – thus Hofner's claim that its own violin bass was developed independently is reasonably plausible, although it is significant that the 30" scale length chosen for the Hofner bass is identical to that which Gibson used as standard. Otherwise, the two violin basses had little in common; the Gibson instrument was made of solid mahogany, while Hofner's violin bass, like the German company's guitars and violins, was hollow bodied, made of maple and spruce. More significantly, the Hofner version was cheap; at DM344, or $82, it cost a fraction of the price of the few American instruments that were imported to Europe.

The construction of the violin bass, which Hofner designated by the catalogue number 500/1, was similar to that of the violins and guitars which the company was producing in the '50s. The back and sides of the instrument were made of laminated maple, while the top was made of spruce, solid on early models, laminated on later ones. When Hofner started making guitars, European truss rod technology was extremely primitive, and

Main shot: This post-1964 model features humbucking pickups
1. Designed before the advent of reliable truss rods, the bass features a laminated neck for extra strength
2. On/off switches for each pickup make it easy to turn the sound off by accident!

1

some of their early guitars dispensed with this feature altogether; hence early instruments featured laminated necks for extra strength, made from maple and rosewood.

The Hofner violin bass's hardware was basic, to say the least. There were many variants over the years, but the best-known, post-1964 model featured two humbucking pickups made locally for Hofner, and a plastic control plate on which were mounted volume controls for each pickup and three sliding switches. This plate (which according to the customary gimmick-ridden '60s sales literature was termed the 'double-plate flick-action console') was, like the guitar's scratchplate, made of pearl-style celluloid; two of the sliding switches turned each pickup on or off, while a third, termed 'rhythm/solo' offered a preset '70%' volume reduction. The bass featured a simple trapeze tailpiece, while the bridge was made of black-stained slotted wood; short sections of fretwire positioned in these slots acted as bridge saddles. This arrangement was also used on most of Hofner's arch-tops, and provided for simple intonation adjustment. The machine heads were a cheap, open-back type; with small cogs and buttons these gave a lot of backlash (the keys can be turned some way before affecting the tuning) and are not particularly durable.

Although technically the Hofner bass is positively antediluvian, its light weight and distinctive sound make it instantly attractive. It provides the diametric opposite to a modern bass sound, with a thuddy warm tone which has a lot of depth but a lack of attack to the note and no real ring; comparing it to a modern bass is like comparing a double bass with a piano. Its short scale length contributes to a muddiness on low notes, but makes it easy to play; however, although the sound might be 'low-fi', it records easily – where a Steinberger's treble response might make it sound thin on tape, the Hofner sounds woody and solid; just like a Beatles record, in fact. Recording a Hofner with heavy compression gives a more even, less 'thuddy' sound – listen to 'Paperback Writer' for an example – which sits into a mix very easily.

Is it possible to divorce the inherent qualities of the violin bass from its position in history? Probably not. That doesn't make it any different from any other significant electric guitars, all of which had to wait for a celebrated exponent before they became acknowledged as classics. The violin bass has also become so synonymous with Paul McCartney that it's impossible to imagine a musician who hates The Beatles playing one! Fortunately for Hofner, that species is rare enough to ensure that this instrument was their most successful model; although the rest of their range bears little relation to the guitars the company produced in the '60s, the violin bass remains in production today.

2

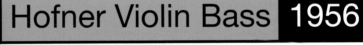

Hofner Violin Bass | 1956

'In the shopping area in the centre of Hamburg there was a little shop near a big department store. Fenders even then were around £100 and **all I could afford was about £30 – and for that I found this little violin bass.** I was left-handed and it looked less daft because it was symmetrical. So I got into that and it became my main bass.

'The one I have now is from the last Beatles tour. Even though it was little and cheap it had an amazingly deep sound, and I'm still chuffed that I use it quite regularly now. It's very light, you can walk around and move around, and it actually alters your playing. You play a lot faster, very easily. So I've got right back into it.' *Paul McCartney*

Main shot: The Fuzzface,
so-named for obvious reasons...
Left: Early Marshall 50 Watt head
– and one of its best known exponents

IN OUT

VOLUME FUZZ FACE FUZZ

ER · ENGLAND

In Search of Volume:

Guitar Amplification

If the '50s as a decade belonged to the guitar designers, then the '60s (especially in Britain) belonged to the amplifier designers and effects-unit manufacturers who worked to expand the electric guitar's palette of colours and satisfy the craving for ever-greater volume and heavier, more distorted sounds. In doing so, they defined the classic sounds of rock and made the guitar a more expressive instrument.

Many advances in the '60s sprang from direct collaboration between electronics experts and star players. For guitarists at the leading edge, custom 'tweaks' and circuit re-builds were the order of the day, with open-ended experimentation in the studio producing distinctive results. But the bespoke one-offs of this innovative decade became the standard models of the '70s, allowing the new sounds and textures to be achieved consistently by any player – often at modest cost.

One change in particular turned out to be highly significant. Distortion textures – whether generated by the amplifier, add-on fuzz-boxes, overdriven speakers or a combination of these – became a vital part of the guitarist's language. Until the '60s, no electronics designers in their right minds would have wanted to add a crunchy 'edge' to hard-picked notes, or turn a crisp chord into an aggressive, rasping fuzz or smoothly sustained buzzing sound. So the Fender or Vox amplifier of the late '50s/early '60s was built to sound as clean as a whistle under normal playing conditions, and it was a very crisp, clean and cutting guitar sound which stars like Buddy Holly and The Shadows had engraved on the public's imagination.

Yet controllable distortion represented a major advance. The ability to shape texture and dynamics from one note to the next was a key element in the performances of players like Jimi Hendrix and Eric Clapton. And while greater on-stage volume was obviously of practical importance, it was also part of the search for that distorted and sustaining sound. Some sections of an amplifier's circuitry would only give useful overdrive if run flat-out, which meant setting all the controls (including volume) on 10 and controlling the sound from the guitar – in the studio, as well as on stage.

It was only later that master-volume circuitry on standard models allowed the player to use a high-gain preamplifier setting for a raunchy sound but run the power amplifier section at a modest level. Physical loudness was also helpful in the controllable-feedback department: by the late '60s, harmonically-related feedback tones (and sustained notes which grew instead of dying away) were a regular part of the heavy guitarist's repertoire. Choice of guitar was part of the sonic equation, too. Late-'50s Les Pauls and early ES335s became favourites because their humbucking pickups would easily overdrive amplifiers like the Marshall 50-Watter;

in the '60s

the main alternative was the Stratocaster, plus a fuzz-box to compensate for the lower output of the single-coil pick-ups.

Almost all the influential designs of the '60s retained valve circuitry; transistors played a vital role in the development of small, battery-powered effects units, but couldn't equal valves in providing the tone, distortion and touch-sensitivity that pro guitarists expected from their amplification. And while effects like spring reverb, tremolo and vibrato were common in early-'60s amplifiers, they were usually dropped from those British heads (such as Hiwatt, Marshall, Orange, Sound City and Simms-Watts) intended first and foremost to be gutsy and loud. Against this, the newly-introduced wah-wah pedal (an active, foot-operated tone control) allowed the player to create a variety of effects including 'talking guitar', while frequency-doublers and tape-echo added extra colour to the signal.

In catering for greater on-stage volume, the amp-makers also provided an impressive backdrop of man-sized speaker cabinets. By the late '60s, no progressive player would be seen without a Marshall stack – a far cry from the days when a whole band (including vocalist) would plug into a Vox or Fender combo at the front of the stage.

A series of musical episodes propelled this 'more-gain, more-volume' trend. Early amplification had been as much to do with accordions and lap-steels as the conventional electric guitar. Then came rock'n'roll, the beat boom, the 'British invasion', the blues boom, heavy rock and heavy metal – with the adrenalin level, volume level and size of venue rising each time. A series of milestones stand out: 'Rock around The Clock'; 'Apache'; The Beatles at Shea Stadium; The Yardbirds' singles; 'Satisfaction' (with Keith Richards originally dismissing the track's prominent fuzz-tone as 'a gimmick'); the *Blues Breakers* album; Hendrix at Monterey; Ten Years After at Woodstock; Led Zep's first two albums... Each produced a multitude of guitarists hankering after 'that' sound.

But it wasn't actually the '60s players who devised the sustaining, distorted sound. Through the '50s, black guitarists playing electric blues and R&B in America's industrial cities had been discovering what happened if you wound up a small combo to full volume and played in an impassioned way. The extra 'edge', sustain and compression made for a more exciting sound, with Fender guitars producing a stinging tone, and humbucker-equipped instruments giving a fat, rich sound. When the records of these supposedly 'minority' artistes catering for 'local audiences' arrived in Britain, a whole generation of white musicians were turned on by what they heard – and they soon re-exported the music of B.B. King, Buddy Guy, Freddie King, Chuck Berry and many others back to the US, completing the circle.

The Marshall Sound

The Vox brand typified many of the design changes through the decade. In the late '50s, their flagship was the AC15, a 15-Watter with single speaker. Then came the 2x12 AC30 (with top-boost option for more gain and punch), followed by the AC50, AC100 and 4x12 cab. At the heart of the story, though, is the development of Marshall amplification. As with many advances, this wasn't a clear-cut case of a revolutionary design coming out of the blue, to meet a well-defined but unfulfilled need. The earliest models, emanating from Jim Marshall's West London music shop in 1962, clearly capitalized on the strengths and popularity of Fender amplification, though the brand soon established its own identity.

Ken Bran was the young electronics engineer who oversaw the introduction of Marshall gear, and looked after the technical side of the operation for many years until retiring as Deputy Managing Director (under Jim Marshall) several years ago. He recalls the birth of the brand:

'I was working as a service engineer at Jim's shop, repairing and rebuilding guitar amplifiers. Selmer and Vox were the most popular brands at the time, though we also stocked the imported Fender range; these were the "in-thing" but very expensive. The most sought-after Fender was the Tremolux but I particularly liked the Bassman, which I came across when a customer brought one in for repair. It had a different harmonic structure to the others – the audio response had a hole in the middle, giving a nice "stretched" sound, and it was a beautiful-sounding combo for guitar – though ironically, not for bass!

'I suggested that we could build an amplifier along these lines far, far cheaper than buying it in from the States. Together with a friend of mine, Dudley Craven, who was an electrical apprentice at EMI, I pondered the possibility of building a version of the Bassman using all British parts.

Dudley and I had often collaborated on ham radio projects, and we worked together on the prototype. The RCA output valves were the only parts in common with the Fender, and the use of different transformers and passive components meant that ours sounded quite different. Firstly – this was the biggest improvement – there was more gain; secondly, it had a different tonal signature: our transformer had more iron in it, so gave richer harmonics, especially at low frequencies.

'For safety reasons we went to a 2½" rather than 2" chassis on production models, but other than getting round the problem of the erratic supply of some parts and upping the power slightly, there wasn't any major development work to be done – we had a distinctive product which was well-received in the shop. Initially, no one had actually been asking us for more gain or a richer sound, but experienced players like Pete Townshend, Jimmy Page and Cliff Bennett's guitarist [Mick King] soon learned to use that thick, distorting sound to good effect. And less expert players – who often had to rely on cheaper guitars with poor pickups – found that our amps beefed up their sound. Either way, once guitarists tried the extra gain, they found they liked it. And once the process of upping the gain and power was under way, it took on a momentum of its own, with people like Pete Townshend and later Ritchie Blackmore always pushing for more – often to the very edge of what was technically feasible.

'We soon went over to English 6L6 valves, which increased the power to 45 Watts, and by 1965 we were building the first 100-Watter for The Who. For the latter, we opted for solid-state rectification and four 6L6s, but these valves were pushed too hard; the output valves were always the weakest link. After various trials, we ruled out transistor technology on sound grounds, and in early '66 went over to EL34 valves; this also solved the earlier valve supply problems. The original model followed suit and also gained solid-state rectification, becoming a 50-Watter; I had been reluctant to alter the circuitry, but there was no drastic change in sound – a little more hardness, perhaps. And the 100-Watter was a big success, even though it sounded brighter than the 50-Watter.

'At this stage, we were liaising with many top players. Hendrix used to come into the shop, for instance. We'd meet him on a gig, he'd tell us what he wanted doing, and we'd make it up for him at the factory. Later he'd call in at the shop to collect it, and perhaps also buy one or two stock models while he was in. Much of what he used was stock, but the ones which were built specially for him had extra gain in the pre-amp. That's what he was after; he wasn't bothered about tweaking the power output. In fact, he preferred the sound of the 50W to the 100W; when he had the choice he would link 50-Watters rather than using 100-Watters. Ritchie Blackmore was the opposite; he preferred the 200-Watt Majors we built later in the decade, and also wanted gain by the bucketload – for him, we took it to the point where you couldn't get any more from a standard amp.

'By the '70s, we faced a lot more competition and chose to meet market demands by adding facilities like master-volume, reverb and split-channel operation on new models. So-called experts (mainly in the States) were charging a fortune to modify our earlier products – often crudely, sometimes even dangerously.'

Ken Bran also acknowledges the role of the Celestion G12 speaker in 'the Marshall sound': 'Without Celestion we couldn't have accomplished half of what we did. At the very beginning, we used Goodmans hi-fi speakers, but I soon got Jim to change over to Celestion G12 Alnico drivers because their sound suited the guitar so well. Within a few years we were Celestion's biggest customer in financial terms, and many of the changes to the G12 – to make it a more robust speaker – were made at our request. The technological improvements did alter the sound slightly, but we were delighted to see power-handling increased.'

1. Marshall 4x12 with *Blues Breaker* combo (foreground)
2. The Beatles' USA tour 1964 – with just three Vox amps, they travelled light
3. The first Marshall prototype, derived from a Fender Bassman

By the late '70s, the 100W channel-switching 1x12 combo was a reality, and the practice of 'miking-up' through a big PA was giving guitarists the freedom to choose whatever format they felt most comfortable with on-stage. Sheer power had become less important than the ability to switch between the three classic sounds ('50s clean, early-'60s 'crunch' and late-'60s heavy-distortion) at any volume-level. The familiar wall of 100W heads and 4x12s was redundant, though many heavy bands chose to keep up their 'machismo' image – even if many of the cabs were simply dummies... And just as a fuzz-box was once the accessory to own, so it was now 'de rigueur' to be seen tap-dancing your way along a whole string of floor-pedals: phasers, flangers, echo units, distortion boxes, wah-wah and volume pedals, and so on. Phasing and spring reverb became the prime candidates for in-built effects (to be overtaken later by stereo chorus and, more recently, digital reverb).

In the '90s, with the music shops full of versatile solid-state combos and digital multi-effects units, the valve sounds which powered the '60s are still very much in demand, and vintage amplifiers – original or reissue – are an important part of today's market. Our story is thus a circular one. The search for greater volume, inextricably bound up with the quest for heavy distortion, turned into a search for versatility and convenience. This in turn led many players back to where the process started in the late '50s, with a healthy concern for tone, dynamics, natural valve overdrive and the inherent character of each guitar/amplifier/speaker combination. Which is no bad thing, given that all digitally-processed, ultra-high-gain guitarists tend to sound the same.

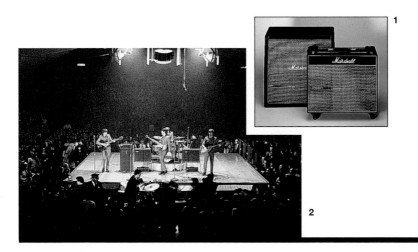

Fuzz-boxes, wah-wahs and beyond...

A fuzz-box is a battery-powered, solid-state distortion device, used between guitar and amplifier. One of the first to be marketed on a commercial scale was the WEM 'Pep-Box', dating from 1963; it was advertised on Radio Caroline, and a later promotional leaflet for the two-knob device quotes a price of '12 guineas' and states 'as used by The Animals and Zoot Money'. Charlie Watkins of WEM remembers the effect that his and other early fuzz-boxes had: 'They hit the scene like a bomb, and everyone wanted one. It was an exciting sound – as if your speaker-cones were being torn apart – but it was quite unlike preamp distortion, because the transient at the start of each note disappeared. At the time, there was no other way of getting this effect, and we were selling hundreds of units through the shops.'

Some amplifier manufacturers weren't too keen. Ken Bran of Marshall: 'When I first heard a fuzz-box, I thought it was atrocious – far too harsh. But the effect grew on me, and we came to realize that the combination of fuzz-box and Marshall amp could work well, provided the player found the right balance between gain on the effect-unit and gain on the amplifier. Within a few years, a lot of groups were using this combination.'

One of the key figures in '60s effects-units was Roger Mayer, an electronics engineer who combined his day-job (Admiralty research in London) with a career building and modifying fuzz-boxes, wah-wah pedals and more exotic effects. Four years after making his first fuzz, he was working with Jimi Hendrix on the *Axis: Bold As Love* studio sessions, and it was his space-ship-shaped 'Octavia' frequency-doubler which helped make the solo in 'Purple Haze' so distinctive.

'My first fuzz-box was built for Jimmy Page in 1963, and the following year Big Jim Sullivan used one of my units on "Hold Me" and "Together", which were big hits for P.J. Proby. To the best of my knowledge, "Hold Me" was the first chart record to feature a fuzz-box, although I remember that the Gibson Maestro was available when I designed mine.

Thanks partly to Page's session work, Roger Mayer's units – one-offs rather than branded products available through the shops – were soon heard on records by many popular acts, including: Dave Dee, Dozy, Beaky Mick and Titch; The Pretty Things; Carter Lewis and The Southerners; and, of course, The Yardbirds. Peter Frampton and Steve Marriott were also keen customers. Mayer made several types of fuzz-box, with different characteristics, and refutes the suggestion that all early fuzz-boxes were just crude 'trigger' devices:

'No, my units were amplifiers – but amplifiers designed to distort in a certain way. The type of transistors used had a crucial effect on the sound. The very earliest fuzz-boxes (including mine) used germanium transistors, because these were more widely available and a lot more affordable than the new silicon transistors; in 1964, each silicon device cost a week's wages (around £6) although the germanium alternatives were still a substantial 7s 6d each. Players grew to like the tone of the germanium-based designs, but later in the '60s, popular units like the Dallas-Arbiter "Fuzz Face" went over to silicon. The result was a less rounded tone, and gain which went right up into the RF band, giving problems with interference and squealing. But both types were useful to guitarists, and I chose to build both – and still do, in the modern versions of my original units.'

Roger Mayer's work with Hendrix highlights the fact that mass-produced solid-state electronics were far from consistent in the '60s: 'I used to rebuild Jimi's wah-wah pedals for him. With each brand, whether Vox or "Cry Baby", there was quite a spread in production, with the sound and the actual wah-wah effect varying from sample to sample. So we used to identify the best-sounding sample, then I would measure it and rebuild the others to make them all as good. As regards hearing wah-wah on record, the first example I remember in the UK was Cream's "Tales Of Brave Ulysses" from *Disraeli Gears* in 1967.'

Folklore has it that in the early '60s, recording guitarists tried all sorts of things to squeeze a bit more distortion from their amps, including slashing the speaker-cones with razor blades. Roger Mayer puts this neatly into perspective: 'None of the musicians I worked with at that time could afford to ruin good speakers! A few players opted for a small additional amplifier in series with their combo, and I made some boosters along these lines. But in the main, if you wanted a fuzzy sound, you either got yourself a fuzz-box or turned your Fender/Vox/Selmer up full.'

And Charlie Watkins bears out the point about small amps: 'For his early recordings, such as the *Undead* album, Alvin Lee of Ten Years After ran his Gibson 335 into our little Westminster combo to achieve his overdrive tone, then sent the signal on to larger amplification. The Westminster produced about 8 Watts from an ECL82-driven power-stage; Alvin particularly liked the sound of this circuitry, and combining the two amplifiers gave him extra possibilities when recording.'

Below left: rare shot of Hendrix with Les Paul, Fuzzface and Vox wah-wah. The Vox wah-wah has now been reissued (bottom left)
Below: Pete Townshend and 'dummy' Marshall cabs (don't try this at home, readers)

On Sunday, 18 June 1967, the electric guitar was, to all practical purposes, **reinvented.** On that occasion, the Monterey Pop Festival played host to a British band called the Jimi Hendrix Experience, led by an expatriate African-American guitarist named Jimi Hendrix.

Hendrix opened his Monterey show with an old blues standard, Howlin' Wolf's 'Killing Floor', but he launched it with a barrelling funk riff that bounced around like a hand grenade in a pinball machine before the rhythm section crashed in. It was a new way of playing an old song: a vintage bottle which could barely handle the strain of containing the combustible new wine with which Hendrix had filled it. Similarly, another blues standard, B.B. King's 'Rock Me Baby', became an uptempo soul stomp which wouldn't have disgraced Wilson Pickett or Sam & Dave. Even Bob Dylan's 'Like A Rolling Stone', a song so venerated that most performers would never have had the presumption to reinterpret it, yielded to him: Dylan's bile-drenched caw became the sardonic amusement of a street-wise black man; those familiar chord changes were filled out with everything from Curtis Mayfield's lilting R&B trills to Pete Townshend's sledgehammer powerchords and the sweet astringency of King Curtis's tenor sax.

Linking the songs with stoned, euphoric babble and powering them with tossed-off runs that seemingly alluded to every sub-genre which rock had ever pillaged, Hendrix alternately charmed and terrified his audience. Rock fans were not altogether unused to black artists: they had seen soul stars both funky (James Brown, Wilson Pickett) and smooth (the Motown stars), they might have seen a few old-style bluesmen or jazz artists, but no black man had ever come on to their turf. The rule until then had been that black artists created and white artists transformed, but here was Hendrix, drawing on both the black originators and the white revisionists and stamping a uniquely personal identity on to everything he touched. This, after all, was the man who made Eric 'God' Clapton go out and get his hair permed.

Hendrix's guitar of choice was Fender's Stratocaster, an unfashionable instrument in the mid '60s since it was primarily associated with skinny, bespectacled nerds like Buddy Holly and The Shadows' Hank Marvin. Within seconds, all that had changed. When subjected to unprecedented levels of pre-amp gain (from the Marshall amps that Hendrix had insisted on shipping to the States, while the Who had unwisely consented to making do with rented Fenders), the Stratocaster's clean, sharp sound became a rich, throaty roar, and its eminently abusable tremolo (vibrato, to be more accurate) system enabled Hendrix to bend and smear notes and chords to sound like anything from a country bluesman's wail to the commencement of the Third World War. Even the crackling of a dodgy or badly screened pickup could be incorporated into an improvisation which preceded the climactic 'Wild Thing'. No one in America had ever heard anything like it.

Forty minutes after walking on stage, Hendrix wound up the proceedings by demonstrating – in the most graphic manner possible, burning and smashing his equipment – that all these guitars and amps and microphones were simply bits of technology. What really made the sounds wasn't a Fender guitar or a Marshall amp, but Hendrix himself. He never designed a guitar or an amplifier, but he knew how to drag infinitely more out of them than the inventors put in.

Hendrix at Monterey

87

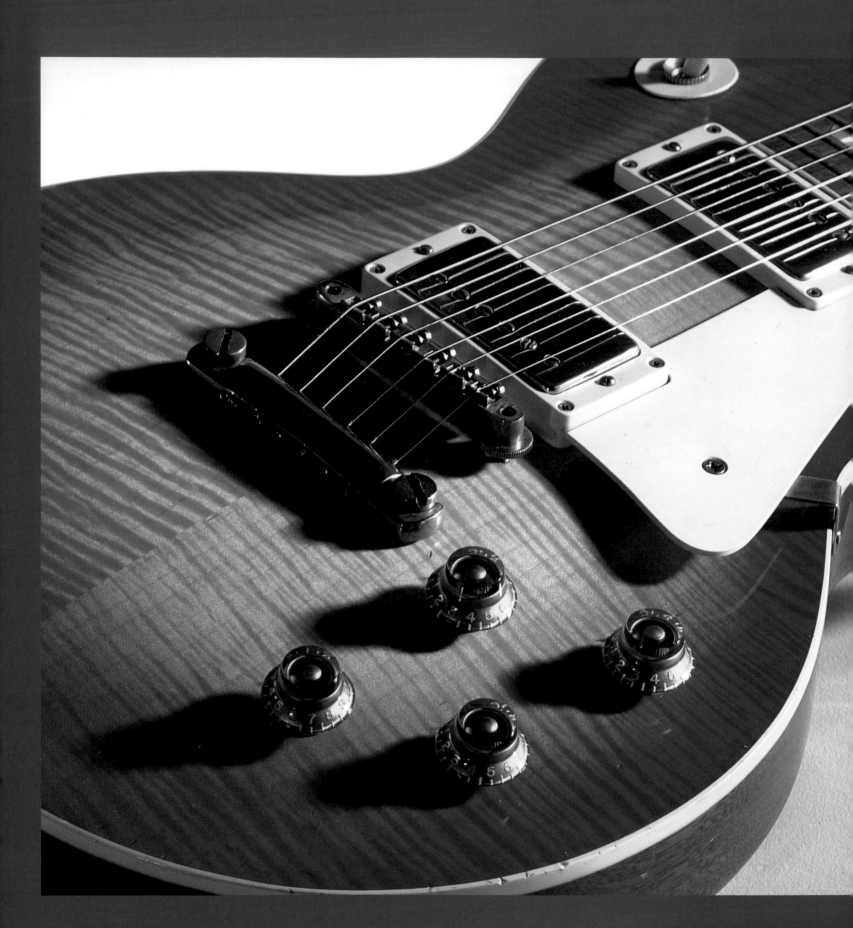

Gibson Les Paul Standards of the late '50s are probably the ultimate rock guitars. They now fetch among the highest prices of production electrics, and in the guitar world are accorded the veneration commanded by Stradivarius or Guarnerius violins. Yet Gibson introduced the Les Paul with some reluctance, made significant errors in the design of the first examples, and dropped the guitar after only eight years in production.

On its introduction in 1952 the Gibson Les Paul attracted much controversy – the then Gibson president Ted McCarty has described how he received a phone call from Fred Gretsch, deploring the fact that Gibson had moved into solid bodies. Yet in many ways this guitar was conventional, resembling their existing ES295 electric acoustic in shape, and featuring hardware drawn almost exclusively from their current models. The guitar's solid body was a radical departure for Gibson, although in this respect they were simply jumping on the bandwagon that Leo Fender had set rolling. Yet the way in which Gibson re-interpreted this concept resulted in a classic guitar that was a combination of Gibson's heritage and new-fangled ideas.

Even today, a vintage Les Paul boasts a sound and feel that most modern guitar makers struggle to match. Its humbucking pickups and solid construction provide a beefy sustain that has been exploited by players from Eric Clapton to Slash, while the translucent flamed maple top of choice early models has acquired a mythology all of its own.

Gibson Les Paul Standard | 1958

Pioneering solid body carved top electric guitar

Les Paul Model introduced 1952

Les Paul Standard released 1958

All Les Paul models discontinued 1960

Modified version reintroduced 1968

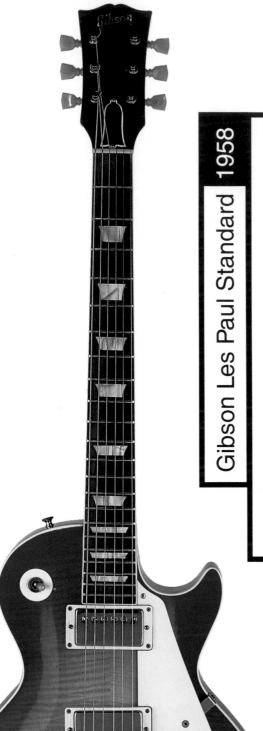

The original Les Paul Model, as it was called, featured the now familiar features of a mahogany body with a carved maple top, a glued in mahogany neck with rosewood fingerboard, and two pickups with volume and tone controls for each pickup, plus a toggle pickup selector on the upper bout. However, although Gibson used a trapeze bridge/tailpiece based on a design by Les Paul, on the early models the company made the error of wrapping the strings under the bar, rather than over, preventing the guitarist from being able to damp the strings with the right hand. Gibson rectified this mistake with a wrapover bridge/tailpiece and new neck angle in 1953.

The Les Paul Model underwent several changes before developing into the Standard – the classic of the breed. It was introduced with a gold metallic finish, and was fitted with P90 pickups; brash, gutsy single coil pickups that Gibson had been using since the '40s. In 1954 Gibson introduced the up-market, all-black Les Paul Custom, which had a separate tailpiece and 'tune-o-matic' bridge designed by Ted McCarty; the Les Paul Model (which is now known as the 'Goldtop', for obvious reasons) gained that arrangement shortly afterwards, and in 1957 Gibson fitted 'humbucking' pickups, designed by Seth Lover.

In 1958 Gibson dispensed with the gold finish, exposing the maple of the guitar's top, and re-named the guitar the Les Paul

1

2

Main shot: 1960 Les Paul Standard
1. 1958 Les Paul Custom – the luxury model
2. 1957 Les Paul Model with goldtop

Standard. It is the Standard which has become known as the ultimate Les Paul; it combines rarity, good looks, and, courtesy of its humbucking pickups, the definitive Les Paul sound.

Although the initial impetus for the Les Paul came from the Telecaster, the Les Paul Standard differs in almost every respect from its Fender contemporaries. In order to differentiate their guitar from its slab-bodied revival, Gibson used a carved arched solid maple top. According to Ted McCarty, 'Leo's Telecaster didn't take much to build – all you needed was a bandsaw. We wanted something that had the quality of a Gibson, and we knew that having a carved top was something that Leo just wasn't tooled up for'. But what had started off as a marketing gimmick gave the guitar a unique sound; the combination of a hard maple top, combined with the one piece body of relatively soft mahogany, and glued in mahogany neck resulted in a warm yet defined tone, with remarkable sustain.

Compared to Fenders, the Les Paul's construction was complex; the tone controls and pickup switch were mounted on to the maple top and accessed via plastic plates at the back of the guitar, all of which necessitated more complex routing. The neck features Gibson's customary back-angled headstock; this provides a good break angle for the strings over the nut but is prone to breakage. For collectors, the maple top of a Les Paul Standard is the major part of its visual appeal, and choice examples boast flamed maple tops.

The hardware also contributes to the Les Paul's weighty sound;

'The guitar I use is the same one that Jimmy Page used. It's a Les Paul Standard – the classic rock'n'roll guitar. 'When I was a kid I used to have the posters on my bedroom wall of Aerosmith, with Joe Perry playing a Les Paul. Let me tell you how that guitar came home to roost.

'I was in Japan and I get this call from a guy saying "I think I've got a guitar you'd really be interested in." So I'm sitting in Japan wondering why anyone would go to such lengths to get in touch with me about a guitar. When I get back to the States this guy calls me again and says something about it being Joe Perry's guitar. So I said "hmmmm" and I know Joe Perry only had one Les Paul and that was a sunburst, a '59 Les Paul and it was one of two and it used to be owned by Duane Allman.

It was the

coolest
guitar
ever,

the way it looked, the sound and everything.

'I didn't believe it at first, but I found out a little background which proved it was true. What happened was Perry had all his equipment sold when he was out of town. It was worth $15-20,000 and it got sold to a pawn shop for a few hundred bucks. The pawn shop sold it to a guitar store in Nashville and they phoned me. So I'm flipping out!

'When I was in high school, any time I opened a magazine Joe Perry was playing this guitar. I paid $8,000 for it and it arrived in the mail. I still can't believe it. It just sounds awesome.'

Slash - *Guns N' Roses*

the bridge is screwed directly into the top, while the tailpiece is bolted via two ferrules. The tune-o-matic bridge is adjustable for overall height and intonation of each string, while the tailpiece is also adjustable for height; this affects the break angle of the strings over the bridge saddles, which in turn subtly affects both string tension and the actual tone of the guitar.

More significant still, in terms of sound, are the humbucking pickups. These were developed by Gibson designer Seth Lover to eliminate electromagnetic hum, but also gave a louder and fatter output, which could overdrive amplifiers more easily. The wiring arrangement for the Les Paul was simple but effective; a toggle switch on the upper bout selected either or both pickups, while each pickup had its own tone and volume control – a more versatile arrangement than contemporary Fenders.

In practical terms the Les Paul Standard boasts few actual drawbacks, but the main reason for its occasional dips in popularity has, ironically, been its distinctiveness – Les Pauls give a fat sound, which is not generally suited to rhythm playing, and which does not cut through lush instrumental arrangements. Playing a vintage model the sound of the lead pickup, in particular, is inspiring; a sweet tone with good midrange strength and bite, which in combination with a good amplifier accentuates the guitar's inherent sustain, which has an almost 'compressed' quality. The neck pickup has a warm mellow tone perfectly suited to blues; the sound of both pickups combined can vary substantially from one instrument to another, but at its best gives a beautiful bell-like tone.

In practical terms the Les Paul is hardwearing, but can be prone to neck breaks; the truss rod is accessed at the headstock, a more convenient method than that of Strats or Teles, but one which requires the removal of a large amount of wood at the neck/headstock junction. Later guitars featured a volute, which added more wood at the vulnerable point.

The Les Paul was expensive to produce compared with Fenders, and was actually regarded as heavy and clumsy when it was first discontinued in 1960. But from the mid '60s an entire new wave of players – among them Eric Clapton – was discovering that the Les Paul's weight and sustain when combined with a Marshall amp perfectly suited the new 'blues boom' sound, and the guitar was reintroduced in 1968. Subsequent years saw huge variations in quality, and although Gibson often boasted that various re-issues were similar to the by-now coveted originals, this was rarely the case. In this respect Gibson almost single-handedly created the vintage guitar market.

The Humbucking Pickup

Seth Lover invented the humbucking pickup in 1957. As its name suggests, the main purpose of this design was to 'buck' or eliminate electromagnetic hum. The development of this pickup was a coup for Gibson, but its success relied on more than its hum cancelling properties. Simply, humbuckers were louder than their single coil equivalents – in the mid Sixties, when guitarists were searching for a distorted tone, this was a huge advantage.

Early Gibson 'Patent Applied For' – or PAF – humbuckers, have acquired almost mystic associations – this is partly due to the fact that earlier pickups had differently-sized magnets and varying numbers of turns in the pickup coils. Their reputation is partly rooted in fact – some later Gibson pickups were definitely inferior – but is mostly due to their rarity. They can be easily identified by the 'Patent Applied For' sticker underneath the pickup, although some forgers have recently perfected counterfeit labels! Some PAFs feature black and white bobbins under the chromed covers, generally known as 'zebras' – these too are favoured by collectors. Gibson's patent was granted in 1959, but their pickups retained the sticker until 1962, when they changed to a patent number.

The SG shape (3) replaced the Les Paul Standard in 1960; despite carrying his name the SG was released without Les Paul's approval. The Les Paul Specials and Juniors were simplified slab-bodied guitars with P90 pickups, designed as lower-priced additions to the Les Paul range. Both the two pickup Special and the one pickup Junior were released in single cutaway and double cutaway form; the model pictured (4) is a 1960 double cutaway Special. Gibson's introduction of simpler, cheaper instruments also resulted in the Melody Maker series (5) all mahogany guitars with thinner bodies and cheaper pickups mounted directly onto the scratchplate, thus reducing costs.

In the mid '50s, the Gibson guitar company were typecast as guitar-making conservatives. Their Les Paul Model had been launched primarily in response to Fender's Telecaster, and, according to the then Gibson president Ted McCarty, 'Leo was going around telling people that Gibson were stodgy and never had a new idea in their life, and that Fender were the guitar company of the future.' The Flying V was Gibson's response.

The Flying V was a piece of sculpture that for the first time acknowledged that the solid guitar could assume just about any shape that took the designer's fancy. When the instrument was unveiled at a 1958 trade show Gibson's dealers were dumbfounded; the guitar was discontinued by the next year. But although the Flying V was a commercial failure, it did achieve McCarty's aim of transforming the image of the Gibson guitar company; they were rarely accused of conservatism thereafter. The Flying V's outline has become far more famous than its sales would justify, and is probably the ultimate expression of the electric guitar's phallic imagery. It's probably for this reason that less exhibitionist guitarists steer clear of the instrument, recognizing that it demands the sexual potency of a Jimi Hendrix or Keith Richards to wear one without looking ridiculous.

Gibson Flying V 1958

First radically shaped electric guitar

Designed 1957

Commercially introduced 1958

Discontinued 1959

Reintroduced 1966

It's well known that the '50s was the decade of car stylists Harvey Earl and Virgil Exner; Earl had added the tailfins of a Lockheed P-38 fighter to the 1948 Cadillac, while Exner had originated the 'forward look', which made the Chryslers he designed look like one big fin on wheels. By 1956 Fender was offering its customers their guitars in Custom Colours – Dupont paint finishes which echoed those in Ford and Chrysler showrooms. By comparison, Gibson's guitars had a distinctly dowdy '40s look about them, with the notable exception of the gold sparkle finish of the Les Paul and ES295. Ted McCarty, whose first major task as Gibson president had been to oversee the development of the Les Paul, set about rectifying matters – with a vengeance. McCarty

was aiming for an angular modern feel like that of the cars of the day, and when one of the design team came up with a triangular shape for the body, he decided to cut away the wood from the base of the triangle to save weight 'and one of the guys said, "That looks just like a Flying Vee!" And the name stuck.' The same team were also responsible for Gibson's similarly angular Explorer, which was produced for the same tradeshow as the Flying V, and the Moderne, of which no authenticated original examples survive.

Although supremely gimmicky, the design of the V somehow worked. Made quite simply out of two slabs of korina – an African limba wood similar to mahogany – the body was simple to produce, much lighter than a Les Paul and surprisingly practical and well-balanced when strapped on, although the addition of a ribbed rubber insert on the treble-side 'leg' of the guitar fails to prevent it from being totally unplayable when sitting down.

Whereas it was Fender's custom to design hardware specifically for each new model they produced, the Flying V used Gibson's new standardized hardware of Patent Applied For humbucking pickups, three-way switch, individual volume controls for each pickup and McCarty's ABR-1 tune-o-matic

Gibson Flying V 1958

Main shot: The Flying V was flashy rather than efficient – but who cares?
1. The guitar was simply constructed with a two-piece korina body and glued-in mahogany neck. The six ferrules visible here anchor the strings at the back of the body

bridge. However, the guitar only featured a single tone control which operated on both pickups, primarily because McCarty wanted a less cluttered control layout for his new shape.

Playing an original 1958 example shows the guitar has a classic sound, despite its gimmicky origins. Unamplified, the Flying V has a lively acoustic ring, which translates to a bright but powerful sound on the lead pickup. The neck pickup possesses monstrous depth, but with a bell-like clarity (on cheaper guitars or copies this pickup can often sound woolly and indistinct). The simple control layout gives a vast selection of different tones, while the guitar's inherent rich and quite long sustain means it's particularly suited to blues soloing, and heavy powerchord work.

The Flying V does not claim to be a practical guitar; at 44" in length it's one of the largest production solid guitars ever, is awkward to transport and, like other Gibsons of the same era, is vulnerable to neck breaks. In commercial terms it was also a failure; Ted McCarty estimates that Gibson made about 80 examples, and similar numbers of its sister model, the Explorer. That first production run took two years to sell and according to McCarty 'a lot of the dealers just hung those up in their shops and didn't even try to sell them.' The poor sales meant that Gibson discontinued the instrument by 1959, although a small number of the original production run were fitted with nickel-plated hardware and released from the factory in the early '60s. The Flying V was reissued in a modified form in late 1966 and by August 1967 had been taken up by Jimi Hendrix who helped achieve a modest revival of the guitar's fortunes; the Flying V was kept in production for most of the '70s and beyond. But the guitar's influence stretched beyond its original sales; in its wake companies like Vox, Burns, Jackson and BC Rich produced angular aggressive-looking instruments, while Japanese manufacturers like Ibanez and Antoria produced straightforward copies. More than thirty years on, it's obvious that the instrument which provoked more derision than any other Gibson design has changed the imagery of the electric guitar for ever.

'I was one of the first guitarists to use a Flying V. **Now they're worth too much money for me to afford,** so I had a guy in Detroit make me a couple of new ones.' *Albert King*

The '70s:

Above: Jimmy Page and trademark Gibson
double-neck
Right: Metal pioneers Ritchie Blackmore
and Roger Glover of Deep Purple

The

Rock music woke up in 1971 with one hell of a hangover. A period of unrivalled creativity had skidded to a halt with the deaths of Hendrix, Jim Morrison and Janis Joplin, and the official break-up of The Beatles in December 1970.

By 1970 the guitar industry, too, seemed in the doldrums. But over the course of the decade the inspiration behind new guitar designs would move from the manufacturers to the players. From simply accepting the products as they came out of the factory, guitarists themselves would begin to dictate the course of the instrument's development.

Fenders and Gibsons had been the chosen weapons of the '60s guitar heroes, but their new products looked distinctly lacklustre. Despite that fact, Fender's Stratocaster and Gibson's Les Paul were established as two conventions which would influence both guitar-players and guitar-makers, their sounds constituting a standard others would follow. But both instruments had their drawbacks – the Les Paul was heavy and cumbersome, while the Strat was difficult to control at high volumes; where Hendrix had coaxed high level feedback and radical tremolo bends from his Stratocaster, the average player found the weak single-coil pickups prone to unmusical squealing and microphony at high levels and wrestled to get the tremolo to stay in tune. Over the next decade, guitar-makers would struggle to combine the strong points of both instruments, and eliminate their shortcomings.

As the '70s opened, most guitarists were still betraying the influence of their '60s forebears. Cream broke up in 1968 but their influence continued to be heard in many blues/rock bands such as Free, whose *Fire and Water* album from 1970 contained some of guitarist Paul Kossoff's best playing. Initially influenced by Eric Clapton and Peter Green, like many whose introduction to the blues came from the British blues players, Kossoff started listening to B.B. King and Freddie King. Although Kossoff also played Strats, he is generally associated with his Les Paul Standard, his interest in the guitar stemming from Clapton and Beck. But Kossoff's career was short-lived; Free split within a year of their first hit single and album, and Kossoff failed to establish consistent form due to drug-related problems which resulted in his death in 1976.

Although new musical strands did emerge in the early '70s, they were not particularly promising ones. In Britain the glam movement threw up several talented artists, including Marc Bolan and the inspired David Bowie, who was accompanied by the stalwart Mick Ronson on platforms and Les Paul. But although Bowie in particular would remain unfailingly inventive throughout the decade, most of his companions in the chart were shallow fodder, who in Britain were mostly the products of two production stables, Bell and Rak, led by Chinn/Chapman and

Mickie Most respectively. Mickie Most had produced many classic songs, including some of The Animals' finest material, but as he himself freely volunteers, 'Most of that music was awful, just watered down versions of '50s music, really. As far as I'm concerned we could have wiped out the '70s entirely, and gone straight from the '60s to the '80s.' The same could doubtless be said for many of the American teenybop acts of the era, including The Osmonds and David Cassidy.

The most enduring symbols of '70s rock, however, were Led Zeppelin, who spearheaded a move towards 'album rock' and a consequent fragmentation of popular music which endures to this day. Although the band exemplified all the overblown excess and self-indulgence of a decade which also saw the advent of album bands like ELP and Yes, Led Zep's roots were based firmly in the musicianship, studio experience and blues influences of ex-session guitarist Jimmy Page. Although the band's first album was recorded with Page using 'a Tele and a battered old Supro amplifier' he soon moved to a Les Paul. 'I got too much feedback with the Tele, and I needed the amplification because Bonzo had so much attack – that made his drums sound so big that you had to have the power there to get the balance between the three instruments. With the Les Paul it was all there, the sustain and stuff.'

Although musicians such as Hendrix had previously spent huge amounts of time experimenting in the studio, Led Zep were the first band to succeed in achieving a truly bombastic sound on tape, hiring three-storey houses and using ambient mikes to achieve, in particular, a huge drum sound which remains influential to this day (so influential, in fact, that it has been regularly sampled, even making its way on to records by the impeccably tasteful Cocteau Twins). According to Page, some time in 1970 Led Zeppelin drummer John Bonham was talking to George Harrison 'and he said "The problem with your band is that you don't do ballads." So I purposely stuck the first two notes of 'Something' on this song ['Stairway To Heaven'].' Page's composition was to become the archetypal '70s rock song – to this day it is programmed several times a week on hundreds of American AOR stations, and it's reported that one Florida station recently played the song back to back continuously for 24 hours...

Do It Yourself Decade

Although regarded by their fans as superior to the genre, Led Zeppelin played a large part in the rise of heavy metal, which started to take distinct form in 1971 with the release of the album *Paranoid* by Midlands group Black Sabbath. Never destined to be a critic's favourite, guitarist Tony Iommi's ominous, grinding riffs inspired many of the New Wave of British heavy metal bands of the late '70s and the American 'speed metal' bands of the '80s, such as early Metallica. Another terminally unfashionable band, Deep Purple, released *Made in Japan* in 1972 – this live album captured Purple at their bombastic best and included the definitive version of the infamous 'Smoke on the Water', an essential riff every fledgling rocker must learn. Like many of their competitors, Deep Purple saw the introduction of classical influences as a new way forward for rock music, going as far as recording a *Concerto For Group And Orchestra* with The Royal Philharmonic Orchestra, conducted by composer Malcolm Arnold, at London's Albert Hall.

Other players set out to broaden the scope of rock music by including jazz elements, in what was termed fusion. An important and influential album in this genre was Mahavishnu Orchestra's *Birds of Fire*, released in 1973, with guitarist John McLaughlin fully exploring the possibilities of the Gibson double-neck 6/12 string. McLaughlin was an intensely dedicated musician and a formidable guitarist. As Frank Zappa commented, 'A person would be a moron not to appreciate McLaughlin's technique.' Inspired by the Mahavishnu Orchestra, the ever-changing off-beat maestro Jeff Beck released his renowned fusion album *Blow by Blow* in 1975.

English rock group Queen were one of the few bands who incorporated classical influences and still enjoyed success in the singles charts. Guitarist Brian May was initially inspired by Hank Marvin and later by Clapton, and anticipated a movement in which guitarists would customize instruments to their own taste by building his own guitar in 1963: 'I was about fifteen when I started building my guitar with my dad. The neck was from an old fireplace and an old oak table was the basis for the body. The rest of the body was blockwood and veneer, with the oak taking the strain. I bought some fretwire from a guitar shop in Cambridge Circus but it was very high, so I made a little jig to cut it down, smooth it out and get the profile right so they wouldn't spring out when we put them in – we went to great lengths!

'The position markers were mother-of-pearl buttons – the tremolo was carved out of a piece of mild steel, and it rocks on another piece of steel plate which we case-hardened. The tremolo rocks against motorbike valve springs and the tremolo arm itself was a saddle bag support from a bike. We designed the tremolo system for as little friction as possible and it worked far better than the tremolo systems used at the time. Originally I made the pickups myself but I wasn't happy with them, so I replaced them with Burns ones, arranged in my own design. It sounds like a cross between a Les Paul or Strat, but with a lot more range than either!'.

Although May's technical expertise was unique (he turned down a job offer from Jodrell Bank's Sir Bernard Lovell in order to form one of his first bands), from the mid '70s many guitarists embarked on a similar DIY approach as American guitar companies started to offer a range of parts.

The DIY Approach | Larry DiMarzio offered a Super Distortion replacement humbucking pickup in 1975 (he'd designed it a few years before). It was a high output humbucker specially designed to distort a tube amp for a natural crunchy tone without using a fuzz box. Players loved it. DiMarzio weren't alone in spotting the potential on the 'bits' market; copies of the concept soon followed from Mighty Mite, DeArmond and Gibson, while Seymour Duncan initially concentrated on winding pickups that sounded like the '50s originals.

Soon DiMarzios were offered on various USA brands – for example B.C. Rich, Dean and Guild – and the mid to late '70s spawned a host of replacement parts companies such as Boogie Bodies, Charvel, Mighty Mite, and Schecter, offering everything from hotter pickups, proper five-position Stratocaster switches, improved machine heads and tremolos, brass nuts, and necks and bodies – often from exotic natural finished timbers. Simultaneously, individual luthiers decided that if Gibson and Fender wouldn't improve on their original designs, then they would do so. US guitar companies like B.C. Rich, Hamer and Dean began to produce a relatively small number of guitars but their influence, especially that of Hamer and B.C. Rich, is quite profound in the early '90s. Hamer's Sunburst guitar was essentially a high-class vintage hybrid, a Les Paul double cutaway Special outline with flat, flamed maple top, twin humbuckers and custom-made Strat style bridge. Bernie Rico took a more radical approach with his first guitar, the Seagull, and further designs through the '70s. Typically, these were superbly crafted, original and visually striking designs, generally using straight through neck construction. The trend for through-neck construction was astutely spotted by Yamaha whose SG2000 became regarded as the first credible Japanese-designed electric guitar. But while Yamaha's entrance to the guitar market might have been unwelcome to the Americans, an apparently more serious threat was appearing with the advent of the synthesizer.

Right: Brian May and his fireplace special
Left: Eric Clapton helped re-popularize the Strat in the late '70s with Blackie, a mongrel guitar assembled from several late '50s models

'I was about 15 when I started building my guitar with my dad.
The neck was from an old fireplace and an old oak table was the basis for the body.'

'Our record and that Ramones three chord trick gave punk its outline – hammering on one chord for two minutes and then into another song. I didn't care for the punk tag – it was wrong, but in the end, who cares? It was just kids with **guitars** and **attitude.**'

Although early electronic instruments such as the Theremin can be heard in the soundtracks to science fiction movies as early as the '50s, the first usable synthesizers were modular units designed by Dr Robert Moog in the late '60s. In 1971 he launched the Minimoog, which was easier to use and practical for on-stage use, and helped inspire a generation of more keyboard-orientated and 'cerebral' bands such as Genesis, Pink Floyd, King Crimson and Yes, although Robert Fripp from King Crimson and Steve Howe from Yes were admired for their considerable guitar talents. But while many of these bands boasted expert musicianship, the spirit of their work was far removed from the rock'n'roll and blues that had inspired them. However, in November 1975 and February 1976, the debut albums from two American acts – Patti Smith and The Ramones – received rapturous critical receptions on both sides of the Atlantic. The punks were about to sweep away the ancien regime.

Bloody Punks Although punk rock was regarded as a mainly British phenomenon, it was firmly rooted in American traditions. 'Punk' initially referred to basic American garage bands like The Standells or The Electric Prunes – glorious no-hopers who responded to the British invasion with lamebrained covers of songs like Them's 'Gloria'. This vital tradition was maintained by The Stooges and The New York Dolls in the late '60s. Ten years later, practically every British punk band would include a Stooges, Velvet Underground or New York Dolls song in their repertoire.

The Ramones were direct descendants of America's original punks, specializing in cranked up two-minute surf songs, and, like Patti Smith and Television sprang from CBGB's club in New York. Tom Verlaine contributed some startling guitar work to Patti Smith's Horses, and was also leader of Television, who enjoyed one of the earliest 'punk' hit singles with 'Marquee Moon', title track of their debut album which would later become a blueprint for a host of British 'indie' bands. According to him: 'That whole New York scene grew out of CBGB's club. All the clubs then were tied to the record companies, so if you didn't have a deal they wouldn't let you play. CBGB's was like this country and western bar, and the owner would let us play on Sundays.

'I guess Horses, the first Ramones album, and Marquee Moon started it up.

**Opposite: The Sex Pistols play the 100 Club, London
Below: Television's Tom Verlaine; despite being labelled punks, his band were virtuoso performers**

Our record and that Ramones three chord trick gave punk its outline – hammering on one chord for two minutes and then into another song. I didn't care for the punk tag – it was wrong, but in the end, who cares? It was just kids with guitars and attitude.'

Simultaneously with this New York movement, a London scene was evolving that threw up the Sex Pistols, The Damned, and later on The Clash. The Pistols achieved notoriety primarily by virtue of their assiduous manager, Malcolm McLaren, but for a short time managed to justify, or even surpass the hype. The band only recorded one album in their lifetime, but *Never Mind The Bollocks* was a fine rock outing dominated by the songwriting of bassist Glen Matlock and Steve Jones's multi-tracked, cranked-up Les Paul. Jones, along with Mick Jones of The Clash, The Heartbreakers' Johnny Thunders and Steve Hunter and Dick Wagner from Lou Reed's '70s band, pioneered a return to basics with Gibson Les Paul Juniors and Specials. Simplistic guitars with, in the Jr's case, just one pickup, they epitomized punk's no-nonsense approach. According to Marco Pirroni, later of Adam and The Ants, they had other advantages too: 'We used to have some real oiks gobbing at us and raiding the stage when we played little venues. One time this guy came straight for me and I laid him out with my Les Paul Jr. It's built like a club – It's the only guitar you could do that with.'

Punk inspired the 'do-it-yourself' indie ethic of 'anyone can form a band and make a record'. Its legacy was the biggest influx of new talent of the decade, including Magazine, Joy Division, The Cure, Echo and The Bunnymen, U2, Simple Minds, Blondie, REM and Talking Heads, while more traditional acts such as Tom Petty and The Cars also sneaked in on punk's coat-tails.

Folk Roots Despite the huge publicity generated by punk rock, many proficient players prospered in the '70s. Ry Cooder, who'd started off playing with Taj Mahal and who could have joined the Stones if he'd been a little more rock'n'roll, enjoyed his first hit album with *Bop Till You Drop* in 1979. Later recordings like *Paris, Texas* (the title track of which was based on Blind Willie Johnson's Dark Was The Night, Cold Was The Ground) would further explore America's folk and blues roots. Other classic American bands like Little Feat, led by the inspired slide guitarist Lowell George, and Steely Dan also enjoyed hit albums right up to the end of the '70s.

One traditionally-based English band which rose out of the London pub rock scene would enjoy more success than any of the '70s punks. Dire Straits mainman Mark Knopfler's clean Strat tone sounded reminiscent of Richard Thompson, his laid-back approach was influenced by J.J. Cale and his vocal delivery was similar to Bob Dylan's (Knopfler later worked with him on Dylan's 1979 *Slow Train Coming*), but he soon refined these into his own unique style. Knopfler's tasteful, clean tone helped to re-popularize the Strat, and his distinctive fingerpicking on the band's first hit, 'Sultans Of Swing', was so influential that amateurish renditions can be heard with infuriating regularity in guitar shops throughout the world.

Van Halen

While Knopfler was uniquely retiring for a rock musician, another guitarist who burst on to the scene in America in the late '70s was a bona fide extrovert in the tradition of Jimi Hendrix. Regarded by many as the most important and influential rock guitarist of the decade, Edward Van Halen created a huge following with the *Van Halen 1* album in 1978. In the States, AOR was dominating the airwaves, making the band's brand of loud-mouthed kick-ass party-down rock'n'roll all the more spectacular.

Although Van Halen claimed to have learned many of Eric Clapton's solos note-for-note by slowing down his record player, the Clapton influence is not immediately obvious in Van Halen's playing. On *Van Halen 1*, Eddie Van Halen revolutionized rock guitar-playing with a combination of new techniques which created a new musical vocabulary – right hand tapping on the fretboard, dive-bombing, natural, tapped and pinched harmonics and a fondness for creating 'weird noises'. Perhaps the most influential technique was right hand tapping, showcased in the 'Eruption' instrumental in which Van Halen 'taps' a note with his right hand in conjunction with two slurred left-hand notes to create a fast, smooth 'diddley-diddley' triplet.

Van Halen also popularized 'dive-bombing' – basically, hitting low 'E' then taking it down as far as possible with the tremolo arm. Hendrix had done this, frequently going out of tune as a result. Van Halen suffered the same problem, and although Floyd Rose was working on a locking tremolo system his design wasn't ready in time for *Van Halen 1*. As Eddie explains: 'On the first two albums I used an old regular vibrato Fender tailpiece with a brass nut. I widened the grooves and added a little oil and it sounded great. After that I ran into Floyd Rose and he showed me his special bridge and nut for keeping a Strat in tune'.

Eddie Van Halen's search for a combination of Fender and Gibson facilities was to prove a huge influence on guitar design in the '80s. In essence, Van Halen popularized the concept of the 'superstrat', building up his own design from Boogie Body, Fender and Charvel parts. His main models featured a single humbucker, usually an original Gibson PAF, which was fitted at an angle in order to line up the pickup's polepieces with the narrower string spacing of the Fender bridge. The wiring was kept deliberately simple, and consisted of a single volume control.

Floyd Rose was granted a patent for an improved guitar tremolo system in 1979. His system featured string locks at both the bridge and the nut for tuning stability, although at that stage Rose's design didn't offer fine tuning at the bridge – thus to retune the clamps had to be undone. The fine tuning aspect was patented in 1985 – essentially the same tremolo that has been fitted to huge numbers of rock guitars since the mid '80s.

Quite what the technique-orientated '80s rock guitar styles would have been like without the Floyd Rose is highly debatable. Of course, as in virtually every other area of guitar design, Floyd Rose certainly wasn't the only person addressing the problems of the Strat tremolo. David Storey's tremolo design was patented in 1984 and was manufactured by Kahler. Unlike the Floyd Rose it didn't use twin knife edge fulcrum points to pivot the bridge but a ball bearing race pivot. The bridge end didn't lock, although a behind-the-nut lock was featured.

Ironically, when Floyd Rose approached Fender to discuss collaboration the company turned down his design. Instead, Rose teamed up with the Kramer company, and the resulting Kramer Baretta, which, like Van Halen's guitar, featured a slanted bridge humbucker, original Floyd Rose trem, single volume control and bolt-on maple neck with either maple or rosewood 22 fret fingerboard, would become one of the most successful designs of the '80s. Kramer – if they didn't really add too much original flavour to the solid body electric – certainly emphasized the power of having an important rock guitar player endorsing a product. By the late '80s, Kramer boasted the USA's best-selling guitar both above and below $500, according to a poll in Guitar For the Practicing Musician magazine.

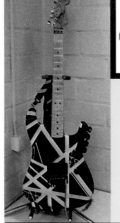 

Opposite: Eddie Van Halen His 'Frankenstein' guitar (left) featured a single pickup and, by 1981, a Floyd Rose trem and nut lock (above)

'On the first two albums I used an old regular vibrato Fender tailpiece with a brass nut. I widened the grooves and added a little oil and it sounded great.'

Above: New wave metallers Iron Maiden

The Heavy Mob Although the group Van Halen represented the more accomplished end of the heavy metal spectrum, in Britain the so-called 'New Wave of British Heavy Metal' (NWOBHM) matched the energy of punk with altogether different influences and aspirations. The two most noted survivors are Iron Maiden and Def Leppard. Although taking inspiration from Free, Led Zeppelin and Deep Purple, all bands with one guitarist, both bands had two guitarists in the line-up, and both were to develop their own unique style and reap the rewards in the '80s. Maiden built a style around 'galloping bass', harmony guitars and pseudo-operatic vocal dramatics, whereas Leppard didn't perfect their pop metal formula of highly processed, overdubbed guitars with strong vocal hooks until as late as 1987 with the Hysteria album. Many other NWOBHM bands faded into obscurity but the whole scene was a significant influence on the US bands that were forming in the early '80s, such as Metallica, who paid tribute to these and other influences on their *Garage Days Revisited* EP in 1987.

Although the '70s, the decade of the copy, did not see many new classic guitar designs, significant advances were being made in the manufacturing process by the American company Peavey. Led by the ebullient Hartley Peavey, the company is credited with introducing computer-assisted machinery to manufacture solid body guitars in the USA, in 1978, for the T-60 and T-40 guitars to compete directly with the offshore imports. This allowed woodworking to metalworking tolerances. Above all it gave great low cost product consistency – producing eight necks in nine minutes – and by the early '80s Peavey were producing 350-400 instruments a day, soon becoming one of the largest volume manufacturers of solid bodies in the USA. Peavey's designs were not particularly versatile but were a major breakthrough in achieving consistent quality at a reasonably low price.

Despite an uninspired start to the decade, by the end of the '70s many bands had genuinely expanded on the legacy of the '60s; the likes of Van Halen and Dire Straits would go on to become some of the best-selling acts of the '80s. But the last major band to emerge from that decade had definite roots in the '60s. Posing as bleached-blond punks, The Police were really three eloquent and experienced musicians who saw jumping on the punk bandwagon as a convenient way to draw media attention. Guitarist Andy Summers was an experienced studio and gigging musician whose guitar work helped give The Police their unique sound: 'I try and make the guitar part as interesting and personal as possible.' Summers did this with tasteful use of effects and the discreet application of his considerable theoretical knowledge. Most importantly, this guitarist, who'd gained much of his experience with Eric Burdon and The Animals in the drug-crazed late '60s, and used a simple Telecaster Custom, extolled the virtue of economy. Where his predecessors of the late '60s had often overshadowed their material, Summers' subtle chorussed sound was definitely subservient to the song. In what should be an enduring lesson, Summers emphasized the guitarist's role as musician rather than hero, and for perhaps the first time in popular music, demonstrated that less really could be more.

The Rise of The Copy

Few areas in industrial design exhibit as much conformity as that of the electric guitar. Although Gibson and Fender have historically dominated the history of the solid body electric, the companies themselves have not always benefited from the ubiquity of their instruments. Fender's Stratocaster has become by far the best-selling guitar design of all time; unfortunately for Fender, the majority of guitars bearing the Strat's distinctive shape have been made by the company's competitors.

The story of the copy electric guitar is very nearly as old as the history of the electric guitar itself. Rickenbacker produced their Electro Spanish model in 1933; within five years the Japanese Guyatone company had produced a replica. Although this model was almost unheard of both inside and outside Japan, it was a clue to how quickly the Japanese makers would recognize – and imitate – innovation.

The late '50s were the start of the boom times for the instrument, and around the world guitar-makers were working hard to satisfy an ever-increasing demand. America was the home of rock'n'roll, and American guitars were naturally regarded as the ideal tools of this new trade. However, they were expensive and still hard to obtain abroad, so domestic makers in each country supplied their cheaper variations on the USA theme. They were well aware of the desirability of the real thing, and the commercial potential of instruments that at least looked similar. So, while exact copies were not made at this time, there were various 'strongly-suggestive' guitars, such as the Fender-like Grazioso (later Futurama) from Czechoslovakia, and the Gibson Les Paul-ish Framus Hollywood from West Germany.

In the early '60s this practice became more widespread, and Fender themes began to dominate. Soon, virtually every country was producing a crop of home-grown guitars that bore a general resemblance to (in most cases) the Fender Stratocaster.

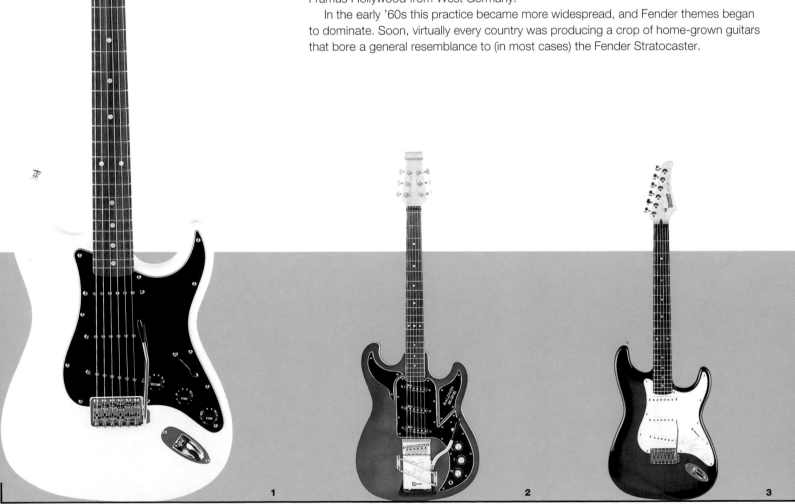

1   2   3

From Britain came the creations of Burns, Watkins and Vox; West German makers included Hofner, Klira and Framus; Sweden and Holland weighed in with Hagstrom and Egmond. Eastern European countries such as Yugoslavia and Poland had their Fender-derivatives, and even Russia was not immune to this all-pervading Western influence. Across the globe, Maton in Australia and Jansen in New Zealand fell under the Fender influence, as of course did Japan. However, although the latter's earliest efforts of the late '50s characteristically bore distinct 'copy' traits, the choice of subject was more bizarre, with many Japanese instruments resembling American-made National and Supro solids. By the '60s, however, the practice of producing close copies of American designs was becoming established.

The first true copies did not appear until the end of that decade, and inevitably these came from Japan. From the first obvious Fender and Gibson lookalikes, the Oriental makers quickly expanded their reproductive horizons, encompassing virtually anything of Western origin, including some of the more obscure instruments: Gretsch, Rickenbacker, Mosrite and even Ampeg models.

The '70s was the decade of the copy – Japanese makers were by now offering reproductions of seemingly every significant American design, while the quality of American models suffered as accountancy procedures took priority over craftsmanship.

Early Japanese copies frequently aped the looks, rather than the construction, of American originals. Fender designs, optimized for mass production, were often copied accurately, but the glued-in neck, carved top construction of Gibson Les Pauls was often ignored so that Japanese copies had bolt-on necks, a pressed top which was hollow underneath, and single-coil pickups fitted underneath humbucker-style covers. But Japanese production techniques and standards improved rapidly, and the term 'Japanese copy' soon lost its automatic association with poor quality.

Many reputable Japanese brandnames were founded on the high reputation of their copies, including Ibanez, Aria, Tokai and Fernandes. Such was the success of these models that Fender, in particular, elected to fight fire with fire, licensing their own copies of classic Fender models in 1982 under the Fender Japan or 'Squier'

tradename. Ironically, Fender executives were staggered when they took delivery of the first production samples of these 'low-priced' electrics; their quality was as good as, or better than, the company's American-made vintage replicas. However, since then Japanese factories have, in their turn, been undercut by production sources overseas – most lower priced copies now emanate from Korea and Taiwan.

Even where manufacturers do not set out to produce copies of vintage instruments, they have to tread warily in terms of radical development; and many choose to rely on the best of past designs, allied to new ideas in circuitry and hardware. Thus guitars like the Levinson Blade feature improvements in hardware and circuitry while retaining the Stratocaster and Telecaster shape to provide the player with a feeling of comfortable familiarity. According to some reports, the guitar's sales in America were adversely affected when Levinson changed the headstock shape following pressure from the Fender company – such is the perceived integrity of the Fender outline that even small variations cost sales. European Blades retain the 'original' headstocks, perhaps because Fender have found that protecting their models' design outside of America is prohibitively expensive.

The copy succeeds on many levels. It can enable guitarists to emulate their hero's choice of instrument, at least visually, and in a cheaper package. Playing an expensive-looking copy achieves a pleasing amount of self-deception and poer-group admiration. Insurance is another beneficial aspect; owners of the real thing can keep their guitars safely stored, and use facsimiles for live work,. Lastly, some copies, cheap and basic as they are, are simply good instruments. Canadian guitarist Jeff Healey is a well-known exponent of a Squier Stratocaster, while the flamboyant guitarist Prince prefers a $200 Hohner Telecaster copy. With a $75m recording contract, and worldwide notoriety, one assumes he doesn't use a copy to save money, or impress his friends.

Although copies have the beneficial aspect of providing an affordable introduction to the electric guitar, they have also had the drawback of inhibiting innovation and originality. But for all of the reasons outlined above, the copy instrument will always be in vogue, mirroring fashions in the higher-price originals market, perpetuating the design aspects of the real thing, for the benefit of the player – if not always of the designer.

1. If you can't beat 'em... The Squier is Fender's own 'copy' range
2. This late '60s Burns illustrates the then-current practice of echoing Fender, rather than copying
3. This modern Hohner is a straight-forward Strat copy, apparently identical in all but headstock shape
4. Levinson RH2 Blade incorporates real improvements, but still features the conventional Strat outline

4

The Yamaha SG2000 has been described as 'the most important Japanese guitar of the '70s'. To the casual observer this carved top electric looks elegant but unassuming – hardly the kind of instrument to set the guitar industry in turmoil. But as the first Japanese electric guitar to completely depart from a copyist mentality, and made to a standard that matched or bettered its American competitors, the SG represented an ominous shot across the bows of the Western guitar industry.

Fender and Gibson were in the doldrums in the '70s, their attempts at developing new designs, such as Gibson's RD Artist line or Fender's Starcaster, generally ill-fated. In comparison, the SG2000 was inspired, featuring a blend of tradition, with its Les Paul-style carved top, and innovation – the SG's multi-laminate through neck and 'sustain block' had only been previously seen on expensive custom basses. For the first time, a Japanese instrument had become an aspirational object, and the SG2000's use by high profile players such as Carlos Santana – previously a Gibson endorsee – helped transform the credibility of the Japanese guitar industry.

Yamaha SG2000 | 1976

First significant 'original' Japanese electric
Designed 1974-1975
Commercially introduced 1976
Production life 1976 to date

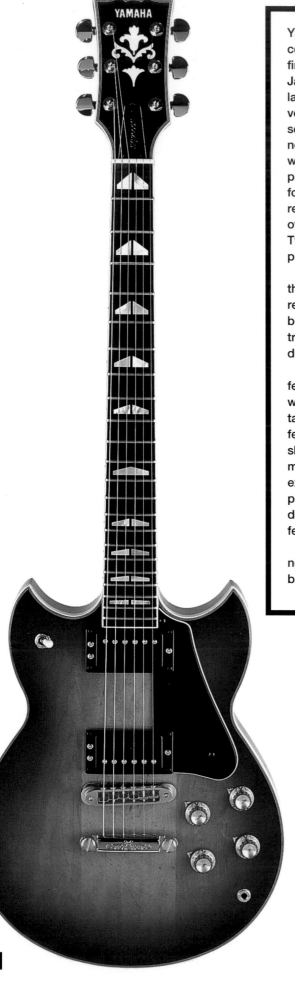

Yamaha was founded in 1887, and made its first acoustic guitar in 1946. The company started experimenting with electric guitars in the mid '60s, and its first production model, 1966's SG2, was a typically eccentric and ungainly Japanese design with a bolt-on neck, and single-coil pickups. Two months later the company released the far more attractive SG5 and 7, slimmer versions of the American Mosrite design, which were well-made and steady sellers in Japan, but hardly ground-breaking. In 1972 the company debuted a new, Les Paul-derived shape; the following year it was replaced by the SG30, which probably marked the first time that Yamaha had succeeded in producing an original design that looked anything but eccentric. This forerunner of the SG2000 featured a distinctive double cutaway shape, which resembled Gibson's SG, but with rounder horns, while the carved maple top of the next year's up-market SG90 was obviously derived from the Les Paul. Two years later a design team headed by the company's Yojirou Takabayashi produced an improved version – the SG2000.

Whereas previous Yamaha electric guitars had followed obsolete trends, the SG2000 was startlingly contemporary. This new model was hardly revolutionary – all of its features had been seen previously on other guitars – but it drew together a number of fashionable themes in a reassuringly traditional-looking package, eschewing the gimmickry of many Japanese designs. It probably represented the first ever subtle Oriental guitar.

The SG2000's debt to the Les Paul Standard is obvious; like that model it features a carved maple top on a mahogany body, two humbucking pickups with separate volume and tone controls, tune-o-matic bridge and bar tailpiece, 24 3/4" scale length, and a headstock which, like '70s Les Pauls, features a 14° back angle. The most obvious departure is the double cutaway shape, which bears a resemblance to some Gibson double-neck custom models of the '50s. Rumours have abounded that Gibson at one time experimented with a double cutaway carved top guitar, even producing a prototype under the Epiphone name; whatever the case, all of Gibson's double cutaway instruments, like the Les Paul Specials or SG range, have featured simple slab bodies.

The SG2000 used a multi-laminate through neck; although by no means a new technique, this was fashionable at the time, particularly with high-priced basses such as Alembics. This construction, which used a central strip of

1

maple surrounded by two lengths of mahogany, avoided the problem of flexible necks and unstable neck/body joints that had plagued Gibson SGs and double cutaway Les Paul Specials. Whereas the Les Paul's body had featured a simple flat back, the SG2000 featured a substantial 'ribcage contour', making it rather more comfortable, and also slightly reducing the weight. The guitar's other departure from the Gibson norm was a brass 'sustain' block set into the maple top underneath the bridge – again, a technique previously used by Alembic.

The result of this blend of old and new was a guitar that felt familiar, and yet was seen as more 'modern' than the Les Paul. The fact that the SG2000 was produced at a time when Gibsons were perceived to have dipped in quality also helped. Apart from its use by Carlos Santana, who had previously featured in Gibson advertisements for the company's L6S solid, the SG range was also taken up by several respected British guitarists, including Bill Nelson, John McGeoch of Magazine and Siouxsie and the Banshees, and Stuart Adamson of Big Country, giving the range impeccable modernist credentials.

In use the SG2000 is well-balanced, if just as weighty as a Les Paul, while the standard of construction is impressive, with a comfortable well-finished ebony fingerboard – sadly, its over-shiny polyurethane finish will never attain the vintage lustre of a '50s Gibson. Although Yamaha designed the guitar to have more sustain than the Les Paul, the acoustic sound of the '70s SG2000S we tested was harder, but rather less resonant than a typical vintage Standard. When amplified the bridge pickup in particular gives a good crisp overdriven tone, although the neck pickup lacks the dig-in-and-wail bluesy sound of a good Les Paul. A common criticism of Yamaha and other Japanese guitars of the '70s were their inferior pickups; those on the SG2000 do sound thin in comparison to a PAF-style humbucker. The guitar lacks character compared with the vintage Gibsons it mimics, but has certainly dated far less than its Japanese contemporaries – or many Gibson electrics of the mid '70s.

The SG2000 has inspired no outright copies, and its sales have remained relatively modest, with 24,000 of the SG2000 and companion SG1000 model produced since its launch. But this guitar paved the way for other credible Japanese designs, and although not always available in overseas markets, has been in production for nearly 20 years. Recently reintroduced to Europe, the SG2000 looks to be headed for a reputation as a venerable classic.

'I used to play a Gibson ES345, but I had it refinished in the late '70s and the tonal quality changed as a result of the restoration. I tried the SG2000 as a substitute and have used them ever since. **I like the no-nonsense, workmanlike quality of the construction;** it's a very strong guitar and can take the punishment of travel, also the tone suited me and the feel of the neck. I think that Japanese guitars are often superior to American guitars these days, although I'd love to have my Gibson 345 back in its original condition.' *Bill Nelson*

Main shot: The SG2000 has obvious similarities to the Les Paul (the model pictured here is the 2000S, which features coil taps on both pickups)
1. Tune-o-matic style bridge mounts onto brass 'sustain block'
2. This shot clearly shows the guitar's through-neck construction; the same laminate section that comprises the neck extends right through the body, with all hardware directly attached to it

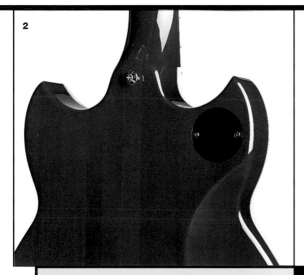

2

Yamaha SG2000 1976

Classic guitar designs of the '70s were about as common as zoot suits at an open air festival. American giants Gibson and Fender plummeted in quality as they struggled to match the low prices of Japanese imports, while the majority of Japanese companies seemed content to plagiarize existing designs. Faced with an uninspiring selection of models in their local guitar shop, guitarists opted for the DIY approach, devising their own instruments from parts offered by a whole new rank of specialist suppliers. Slowly a new concept emerged – that of a go-faster Stratocaster, souped up with more powerful pickups and an improved tremolo.

The Jackson Soloist was the ultimate development of this concept. Grover Jackson's slick combination of elements of both Gibson and Fender concepts was the ultimate heavy rock guitar, its aggression epitomized by a razor-sharp headstock that some hardened metallers found too dangerous for on-stage use! The success of Jackson's design would be ironically underlined by the fact that by the end of the decade both Gibson and Fender would blatantly copy his development of their own designs.

Jackson Soloist | 1981

Pioneering 'superstrat' guitar

Commercially introduced 1981

Floyd Rose option introduced 1982

Production life 1981 to date

The roots of the Jackson Soloist were firmly established in the world of heavy metal. Grover Jackson had taken over a guitar parts business established by Wayne Charvel in 1978. Charvel had developed a line of replacement bodies, necks, pickups and other parts, but sold out to Jackson just as his concept became popular with the advent of Edward Van Halen, who exploded on to the rock guitar scene in 1978. By 1980 Jackson had established a flourishing custom guitar business, and was approached to build a guitar by Randy Rhoads, guitarist with Ozzy Osbourne. Together they developed a model with a Flying V-derived shape, neck-through-body construction, two humbucking pickups and a distinctive pointed headstock. Jackson decided to put his own name on his 'new' design, and when Rhoads established a reputation as one of the fastest young guns on the metal scene in 1981, Jackson's guitars became famous too. His Soloist became established as the definitive superstrat, combining a Strat-derived body with the Rhoads-model's through neck and pointed headstock. Only Kramer's Baretta, which featured a bolt-on neck, but lacked the obvious visual trademark of the pointed headstock, was a serious rival as the definitve superstrat.

Jackson's detractors have openly wondered whether the Soloist actually qualifies as a new design, given that most of its elements were lifted from existing models. Their churlishness was probably provoked by Jackson's extravagant success; if we take the criteria for an important design as being that it is distinctive, and has been subsequently copied by a significant number of companies, then the Soloist is without doubt a classic.

Jackson's concept for the Soloist was a loose one, derived from custom orders – even the 'factory' model of the late '80s was available with a variety of pickups, electronics and finish options. But it established the concept of the Superstrat in the following format.

The Soloist's body is derived from the Strat, with lengthened horns. The neck and centre section of the body are made from one piece of quartersawn maple, with two poplar 'wings' making up the rest of the body – this is a concept taken from Gibson's 1966 Firebird, or even earlier Rickenbacker designs. The fingerboard features 3mm-wide Gibson-style frets and a compound radius, flatter on the higher positions – this retains the 25.5" scale length and feel of a Strat, but enables easier string bending without the strings choking. The most common pickup configuration consists of a humbucker in the bridge position, and single coils for middle and bridge, with a five-way switch, allowing for a combination of Gibson and Fender tonalities. The Soloist, like most superstrats, utilizes a Floyd Rose locking tremolo (which became available as an option over 1982 and 1983, initially without fine tuners) which combines a modified version of the Strat fulcrum device with a nut lock, effectively allowing far more extreme tremolo use.

Lastly, Grover Jackson came up with what is perhaps essential to any 'classic' design – a distinctive visual trademark. His pointed, heavily back-

1   2

'I got into Jackson and Charvel guitars – mainly Soloists – during the recording of Hysteria. **Even the cheap Japanese Charvels** – $300 **guitars – sound great'** *Phil Collen, Def Leppard*

angled head had some similarity to that of Gibson's 1958 Explorer, but was the guitar's most distinctive feature.

Given that the Soloist was developed from a long dialogue with guitarists in Jackson's Custom Shop, it's not surprising that the Soloist is a more comfortable guitar to play than its vintage predecessors. A wide flat fingerboard invites all manner of fretboard pyrotechnics; although anathema to Stratocaster traditionalists, it feels immediately comfortable and permits stringbending even on the highest frets. By the same token, the tremolo system is a development of the Stratocaster's, but permits feats which would be impossible on the Strat trem; a well set-up system will allow the guitarist to bend the strings down to a state of absolute slackness (a facility exploited by numerous metallers intent on impersonating motorbikes), as well as allowing upbends of several semitones. The inclusion of one or two humbuckers also allowed the Soloist and its copies far more scope for distortion than the standard Stratocaster, adding a Gibson tonality that Jackson also aimed to increase with the neck through body construction. Opinion is divided as to whether this actually works; some guitar makers feel that a guitar body which is composed of two 'wings' attached to a central section has a thinner sound than that of a one-piece body with a glued-on or bolt-on neck.

Grover Jackson's creation is, above all, distinctive; whereas the Stratocaster will accommodate a wide range of sounds, the Soloist specializes in heavy rock tones; with a clean amp set up it sounds dull and lifeless by comparison. Cranked up with a Marshall it delivers a definitive heavy metal tone, with more upper mid than a Gibson Les Paul, while the Floyd Rose, although complex, takes the Strat tremolo concept to its extreme, allowing outrageous bends that Hendrix could only have dreamt of.

It would be unfair to judge the Soloist's specialized appeal as a drawback; by accentuating some of the Stratocaster's abilities Grover Jackson chose to forsake others; it's hard to imagine the Soloist in a funk or country and western application. Most of the practical drawbacks revolve around the use of the Floyd Rose tremolo, which although offering excellent tuning stability makes the restringing and retuning process extremely difficult; for this reason, the fashion has lately swung back to simpler systems.

As a souped up, specialized instrument the Soloist is not so much the start of a new design trend, as the conclusion of an existing one. Its influence, however, can be judged by the reaction of Gibson and Fender, who under their tradenames of Epiphone and Heartfield have since launched guitars obviously inspired by Jackson's design.

Jackson Soloist | 1981

3

Main shot: As a mainly bespoke instrument, the Soloist offers a huge range of options in hardware and finish
1. Pointed, back-angled headstock is Jackson trademark
2. Through-neck design enables deep, sculpted cutaways
3. Floyd Rose trem is recessed into body for improved 'upbend'

Launched in 1981, the Steinberger L-2
bass first produced laughs, and then no
small amount of awe. Ned Steinberger's
reinvention of the bass guitar was the most
radical since Leo Fender's invention of the
instrument 30 years earlier; it dispensed
with the headstock, most of the body, and
the traditional guitar-making material –
wood. Although radical, this sleek black
high tech sculpture made from space age
materials won praise from musicians and
design journals alike, prompting its
inventor to declare 'one day all guitars
will be made this way.'

It was not to be. Rather than the
conventional guitar changing to represent
a Steinberger, the Steinberger instead
changed to represent a conventional
guitar. But although commercial realities
forced Steinberger to compromise his
radical design ideals, the concepts he
introduced made an unerasable mark
on guitar design.

Steinberger 1981

| First headless production bass |
| Designed 1978-9 |
| Commercially introduced 1981 |
| Revised 1986 |
| Production life 1981 to date |

Steinberger's story is that of the classic application of industrial design to the traditional craft of guitar making. Like Leo Fender, Steinberger's non-guitar background allowed him to approach the instrument from first principles; as he said at the time, "whether a guitar was a Stratocaster or a Les Paul meant nothing to me – they all looked the same."

From a background in industrial design, mainly for the Thonet furniture company, Steinberger's first involvement in the bass guitar market followed a meeting with Brooklyn bass maker Stuart Spector. Having developed the influential NS range of basses with Spector, Steinberger set out to redesign the instrument from scratch.

Although it would become the most visually striking element of the Steinberger bass, the idea of a headless instrument was not new; veteran guitar visionary Les Paul had experimented with headless models at least ten years before. Steinberger decided to utilize this principle, moving the tuners to the body; having got rid of this literally dead wood he then decided to dispense with the body, too. The resulting prototype, made out of wood, looked almost identical to the eventual production model, but had one drawback: 'it sounded terrible.'

Reducing the mass of the body also adversely affected the sustain. Realizing he needed to increase the rigidity of the structure, Steinberger turned to reinforced plastics. Steinberger experimented with various compositions, before deciding on an epoxy resin reinforced with carbon graphite and glass fibre (the exact formula, developed in conjunction with boat designer Bob Young, is secret). This material was far more rigid and far less resonant than wood; although some amount of resonance can be beneficial, 'colouring' the sound of the instrument on a bass guitar resonance often has the effect of creating 'dead' spots, where the wood's vibration soaks up the energy of the string. Using a smaller, reinforced plastic body eliminated deadspots and gave more attack, more sustain and more definition. This was Steinberger's breakthrough.

Neither the headless design suggested by Les Paul, nor the use of carbon graphite were new – the American company Modulus Graphite already had carbon graphite guitar necks in production; Steinberger had to license the technology from them. But the combination of the two new elements resulted in a totally new design that had distinct sonic and practical advantages over its forebears.

Although strikingly different, the design of the L-2 bass was essentially simple. Neck and body are made from a one-piece moulding ; the hollow

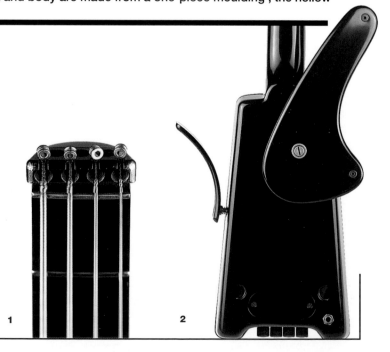

1   2

'I go for sounds not looks, and this bass has that low bass, but it's got the middle and the top you need as well.

Sometimes when I'm playing on stage I might move and hit the tuners, and the bass goes out of tune.

With this one, that's not gonna happen.'

Robbie Shakespeare

body features a lid of the same material, to which the pickups attach while the fingerboard is made of fibre-reinforced phenolic resin with conventional frets. The whole structure utilizes the standard bass scale length of 34" but is only 38" long; at 8lb in weight, it's at least 1lb lighter than most conventional bass guitars, and without the headstock is evenly balanced.

Steinberger's revision of guitar hardware was subtle but effective: the bass uses twin ball end strings; one ball end locks into a recess beyond the nut, the other is clamped at the bridge end by a jaw adjusted lengthwise by a hefty knurled bolt, directly controlling the tuning. With a fine tuning 40 to 1 gear ratio, this method is accurate and practical. Four solid bridge saddles are adjustable for intonation, and can be locked via an allen key.

The Steinberger L-2 used EMG active pickups which further accentuated the bass's clean, 'zingy' sound. EMGs are humbucking pickups with active preamps encapsulated in their black plastic casing; with extremely low susceptibility to noise and interference, and a neutral sound, they perfectly complemented the guitar.

Despite an initial contemptuous reaction to his instrument, Ned Steinberger quickly built up an enviable reputation with the people that mattered – musicians. It's easy to see why. Although playing the L-2 is a disorientating experience for those used to its headed predecessors, its sheer practicality is immediately striking. Tuning the instrument is far easier and more accurate than on a conventional bass, while fitting and tuning new strings (provided you have the correct ones to hand) takes a fraction of the time demanded by most basses. The instrument's balance is perfect, aided by a plastic extension to which the strap is attached, while the L-2's light weight is a further practical advantage.

In ergonomic terms, the L-2 was almost as huge an improvement over its Fender forebear as was the Fender over the 200 year old standup bass design. But the advantages didn't stop there, because the L-2's practicality was matched by its sound; clear but resonant, with a piano-like attack accentuated by the string design. Although less 'woody' than a conventional design, the L-2's sound was just as deep, with a controlled and even sound that was easy to record and amplify.

With all of these advantages, it seems highly ironic that over the next decade Steinberger would heavily modify (some would say corrupt) his design approach – by 1991 his Sceptre guitar design would include a conventional wooden body, and – the horror! – a headstock. It would be easy to infer from this that Steinberger was too radical, or the marketplace too conventional, but this is too simplistic an assumption. Musicians were not conservative – they responded to Steinberger's radical new design with laudatory enthusiasm. The lesson is that there is no such thing as a perfect guitar; any model is a collection of compromises. The sound of the L-2 was

different, but some guitarists simply preferred the sound of a wooden instrument, inconsistent as that might be. The L-2's high price, at roughly $2000 rather higher than Steinberger himself would have liked, restricted its appeal to the professional market. Rather than changing the way all guitars were made, the Steinberger approach became an alternative approach. Since the L-2's introduction other manufacturers, including the British company Status, have independently developed successful headless designs, and both these and cheaper copies have met with commercial success. Steinberger's original model, with minor modifications, remains in production. In a supreme ironic touch, the company is now owned by that bastion of conservatism, the Gibson Guitar Company.

Steinberger 1981

3

Main shot: 1983 L-2 bass
1. Headless design uses 'double ball end' strings which can be replaced in a matter of seconds
2. Detachable mouldings hold the bass in a comfortable playing position
3. This bridge assembly bolts directly onto the body, the four jaws grasp the string ball ends

The '80s:

From Techno-Metal

Tasteful rather than technical: Johnny
Marr (above, with Morrissey), and U2's
The Edge (right)

Thirty years after the birth of rock'n'roll the electric guitarist should, by all logic, have become extinct. The instrument of rebellion was now middle-aged, while its original heroes, if we were to believe Eric Clapton, were more interested in the cut of an Armani suit than in the throbbing sex appeal of an old Les Paul. In America the arrival of 'Gold' radio stations, playing hits of the '50s and '60s, suggested that rock music was strictly an art form of the past, while in Britain bands such as The Human League and Depeche Mode abandoned the guitar for the new, affordable generation of synthesizers.

Perversely, however, the electric guitar was blossoming, with a wider range of musicians using the instrument than ever before. Guitarists like U2's The Edge were developing a new textural approach to the guitar, while a new generation of American guitarists inspired by Eddie Van Halen took a more rigorous, technical line – hell, with musicians like Steve Vai practising up to ten hours a day, they could have made an Olympic event out of it. Blues guitar was enjoying a revival with new exponents such as Stevie Ray Vaughan, while British indie bands like The Jesus and Mary Chain furthered the experiments in white-noise-driven pure pop pioneered by The Velvet Underground. And by the start of the '80s a new crop of guitar designers were actually beginning to expand on what had gone before. Ned Steinberger produced a radical redesign of the electric bass, Paul Reed Smith was working on updating classic Gibson and Fender design principles, while Floyd Rose had developed a reworked Strat tremolo with radically improved tuning stability.

Eddie Van Halen's influence on guitar-playing in America was enormous; his original guitar, decorated with sticky tape, originated a craze for graphic finishes which would endure through the decade; similarly, the rise of the Floyd Rose tremolo, and the 'superstrat' concept can all be traced back to Van Halen's guitar-making experiments. Fender would produce the Lead I electric, which featured a similar single humbucker set up to Van Halen's guitar – it wasn't particularly successful, but Kramer and Jackson, in particular, developed definitive superstrats which would be widely copied. Van Halen's widespread influence even extended to the pure pop field when Michael Jackson asked him to contribute guitar pyrotechnics to 'Beat It'.

to Grunge

Guitar in the High-Tech Era | Significantly, two of 1983's other best-selling singles, David Bowie's 'Let's Dance' and New Order's 'Blue Monday', both employed guitars as an integral part of their sound. Bowie, in a typically astute piece of talent-spotting, recruited the young guitarist Stevie Ray Vaughan to make a substantial contribution to his best-selling single and album in years. New Order were probably the most technically radical indie band of the post-punk era, employing drum machines and samplers, but managed to combine this glossy high-tech style with the throbbing bass guitar of Peter Hook. His heavily processed sound would be frequently copied over the decade.

Despite the fact that synthesizers and samplers were becoming increasingly affordable, such records seemed to demonstrate that the guitar was not under threat. However, the dominance of lush keyboard sounds meant that the first half of the decade saw Fender-style guitars enjoying dominance over humbucking Gibson-style designs – their clearer sound was better able to cut through a synth background than the fatter-sounding Les Pauls. The advent of the synthesizer also had a significant effect on the world of the bass guitar, as bassists found themselves required to mimic or replace bass lines originally played on a synthesizer. Some of these 'synth bass lines' were out of the range of the conventional bass guitar – guitar makers such as New York's Ken Smith solved the problem with the five-string bass, which added a low B to the string complement. The six-string bass was an extension of this idea, adding another string – usually tuned to a high-pitched C – positioned above the normal high G.

Sign Your Name | In the wake of Eddie Van Halen a new wave of musically-literate rock players sprang up in the early '80s, many of whom had a significant effect on the development of the electric guitar.

Randy Rhoads joined ex-Black Sabbath singer Ozzy Osbourne's band in 1980. Rhoads played on just two Osbourne albums before his death in 1982 (the result of high jinks on tour when the plane carrying Rhoads clipped the tour bus it was attempting to buzz). Rhoads's legacy, brief as it was, would prove a heavy influence on the metal fraternity. Rhoads was also one of the first of this 'new breed' to have a signature guitar built for him – the Randy Rhoads Custom, made by Jackson.

Over the same period, Swedish guitarist Yngwie Malmsteen created the so-called 'neo-classical' genre of 'metal' guitar – blindingly fast harmonic minor scales and rippling arpeggios. Malmsteen has so far failed to reach a wider rock audience, but his importance to guitarists was acknowledged by Fender, who designed a signature guitar for him. The Yngwie Malmsteen Stratocaster is unusual in that it features a scalloped neck – like Mr Malmsteen's music, this is an acquired taste.

The rise of signature models was emphasized by Ibanez, whose Artist Relations programme set out to capture the new wave of highly technical guitarists. Their collaboration with Steve Vai, for 1987's JEM range, was perhaps the most significant example – apart from the success of the high-priced signature model, many of the JEM's features were incorporated into the company's RG range. The RG550 has since become regarded by many as the definitive modern rock guitar. Vai also worked with Ibanez on the seven-string Universe – basically a JEM range guitar with a low B string which required special DiMarzio pickups and redesigned Floyd Rose licensed trem. Although the seven-string concept wasn't a new one, the Vai–Ibanez collaboration was probably the first time it could be regarded as commercially significant.

Ibanez also captured Steve Vai's one-time guitar teacher, Joe Satriani, another highly talented player who has managed to make the crossover from a musician fan base to a mainstream rock audience, even without Vai's blatantly 'rock'n'roll' image. The initial results of the Satriani–Ibanez collaboration was a rather conservative version of the 540 Radius, before he too designed his own guitar with wild optional graphics and even an aborted attempt at a chrome-finished body. Fusion player Frank Gambale joined the ranks with the thin sculptured bodied FGM100. More recently the Washburn company showed impressive talent-spotting abilities by producing two signature model guitars with Nuno Bettencourt only months before his rise to fame with Extreme. The signature guitar marks a growing trend in guitar design, reflecting the

modern player's emphasis on technique, greater familiarity with design technology and a desire to discover the 'perfect instrument'.

Innovation Versus Tradition The search for the perfect guitar has generally followed a resolutely traditional route, and of the manufacturers who have attempted to harness new materials in the pursuit of this aim, few have lasted. Dan Armstrong's clear perspex bodied Ampeg guitar certainly had its moment in the early '70s – it was one of the first serious electrics to employ a 24-fret fingerboard (all frets clear of the body) and one of the few electrics to employ a sliding pickup. Travis Bean and Kramer both employed cast aluminium neck constructions for a clean ringing tone – neither found long-term commercial success, nor did Tokai's mid-'80s aluminium-bodied Talbo. Ovation, who had pioneered the synthetic roundback electro-acoustic in the '60s, attempted to do the same with the solid body; the UKII used a plastic body with aluminium frame. Gibson experimented with the Sonex guitar that used a wood chip and resin body with almost laughable commercial results.

New technology has had significantly more success in the bass guitar field. The first known example was that of an Alembic bass made for Fleetwood Mac's John McVie. This used a Modulus graphite neck developed by Rick Turner in conjunction with Geoff Gould – previously employed by NASA – in the late-'70s. The neck was made from fibre-reinforced plastic and moulded as a hollow 'U' shaped section with separate phenolic fingerboard. It offered a high stiffness to weight ratio, didn't require a truss rod, was extremely rigid and stable, impervious to moisture and humidity, and eliminated the dead spots that occur on conventional wooden neck basses . However, the materials are, compared to all but the most exclusive timbers, more expensive, and though employed by a few select manufacturers – Steinberger, Status, Modulus Graphite and Vigier – the commercial appeal, despite the apparent benefits, is small. Integration of graphite strengthening rods into wooden guitar necks is a viable alternative practised by Ken Smith, Roscoe, Vigier (who use a centre graphite neck section without a truss rod) and Yamaha.

By the mid '80s it was becoming 'de rigueur' for guitarists to have their own signature model; Joe Satriani (main shot) and Frank Gambale (top right) had guitars produced for them by Ibanez, while Washburn showed impressive talent spotting by recruiting Nuno Bettencourt (right). Yngwie Malmsteen (left) has his own model Stratocaster with scalloped frets

'Stevie Ray Vaughan helped revitalize the blues scene.

He was a monumental figure,

as important in his own way in the '80s as Hendrix was in the '60s.' *John Mayall*

In the area of composites Ned Steinberger stands out as a beacon of design innovation. In 1981 he premiered the L-2 bass, but despite its endorsement by a range of players from Robbie Shakespeare to Sting, Steinberger would later modify his radical approach, moving, in the mid '80s, to full-size timber bodies for both guitar and bass and in 1991 launching the headed Spectre guitar. Steinberger's deceptively simple design skills extended way beyond 'that small headless plastic thing'! The TransTrem offers a wide travel tremolo that not only keeps the string in relative pitch during bending but also, via a notched gear system, allows the player to retune the guitar by simply engaging the tremolo arm. The TracTuner 12-string bridge allows a single moveable knob to be pulled out and re-engaged to tune any one of 12 strings, all with fine tuning accuracy, while the Sceptre guitar sports a moveable Knife-End Knut to reduce friction, a new tremolo and the Standard Gearless locking tuners. Perhaps because Steinberger has rarely licensed other manufacturers – the exception being Hohner – Ned Steinberger has never achieved the commercial acclaim of, say, Floyd Rose.

However, Steinberger did enjoy more success than Andrew Bond, whose British-made Bond guitar surfaced in 1984 – and sank in 1986. The uncompromising design offered a hollowed, moulded graphite reinforced body and neck, with a saw-tooth stepped fingerboard instead of conventional frets. The control layout included an LED display with pushbuttons. The Bond guitar was a massive and expensive flop; neck heavy, the stepped fingerboard was hard to bend on and the controls were clumsy to use with no advantages over old-fashioned control-knobs.

Instead, the success stories of the '80s were more traditional designs. Paul Reed Smith's guitars have become accepted as modern classics, and have now been copied by countless companies. Similarly, the Music Man Silhouette has slowly gained a reputation with the aid of players like Keith Richards, who has described the guitar as 'the only modern classic'.

The Music Man company had been formed by Forrest White and Tom Walker, who were later joined by Leo Fender. It was later taken over by the Ernie Ball string company, under whose auspices Dudley Gimpel designed the Silhouette in 1986. The Silhouette uses a Stratocaster-inspired body (either ash, poplar or alder) with offset horns; the lower cutaway is deepened to provide good access to the top 24th fret of the maple, six-bolt, fixed neck. The headstock employs four tuners on the bass side, two on the treble side to maintain straight string pull over the nut and reduce the length of a Fender headstock. Although it features a Fender 25.5" scale, like PRS the Silhouette uses a 10" fingerboard radius offering a feel midway between the classic Gibson and Fender models. All the pickups (initially Schaller, now DiMarzio) and electronics are mounted on the scratchplate which can easily be changed to give different pickup configurations. The Silhouette is certainly much more than a Stratocaster copy; it's a more compact, ergonomically shaped guitar that has slowly gained a fine reputation without mass marketing or large player endorsement programmes.

Swiss designer Gary Levinson has also set out to update Fender themes with his Blade guitars; these feature beautifully thought out hardware, including a substantially improved tremolo, with many subtle improvements on the Strats and Teles (and even Jazzmasters) on which his guitars are based. However, some might argue that Levinson's improvements, however effective, are too subtle to qualify his instruments as original designs.

The Low-Tech Approach | The British post-punk boom produced a resurgence in the art of good old-fashioned guitar-playing. David Evans – a.k.a. U2's The Edge – added a new dimension with his heavy use of echo and other effects, although the devices he chose to use were distinctly low-tech ones: 'I stumbled on to an Electroharmonix Memory Man in a shop. I took it down to rehearsals and something about the sound of the thing sparked us all off. It was like adding seasoning to the soup and suddenly we all became aware of all these different flavours in our music which we'd never known existed.' The Edge is not the only guitarist to use a 'texturalist' approach as opposed to the traditional lead vs rhythm approach – other practitioners include Charlie Burchill from Simple Minds, the Farriss brothers from INXS and Andy Summers from The Police.

The Smiths' Johnny Marr rose from the same post-punk explosion as The Edge, although his heroes, such as Nils Lofgren or John Martyn, were from an earlier generation. Marr single-handedly created a vogue for clear, clanging guitar sounds, placing himself firmly in the opposite camp to the

Opposite main shot:
Buddy Guy re-emerged in the '80s with the help of Eric Clapton, shown top left at one of his Albert Hall blues nights
Opposite bottom left: Stevie Ray Vaughan with brother Jimmie
Left: John Lee Hooker, at 83 the most senior citizen ever to enjoy a chart album

likes of Steve Vai and Yngwie Malmsteen: 'There are a lot of closed shop ideas about guitar culture, and I think it's very dated. I've always had a suspicion about the fastest gun approach. I was never the kind of guy who would sit in a guitar shop and run off a series of riffs – to me the guitar was a tool for getting the song across.'

Marr's typically British approach influenced a crop of indie bands from The Wedding Present to Suede, all of whom seemed to share a penchant for basic guitar setups, using Rickenbackers or Fender Jaguars teamed up with basic Vox or Marshall amplifiers. Thus by the end of the '80s it was becoming increasingly obvious that while some guitarists were working on developing the ultimate go-faster superstrat, others were returning to basics.

A new wave of blues players, such as Stevie Ray Vaughan and Robert Cray, boasted distinctive guitar sounds but used a traditional Stratocaster, while Canadian guitarist Jeff Healey won acclaim from many peers, including BB King, and played a cheap Squier Strat copy). These guitarists helped engineer a new commercial viability for the blues, which saw rejuvenated players like Buddy Guy and Albert Collins gaining major label record deals for the first time in years, and playing with Eric Clapton for the well-received 'blues nights' at London's Albert Hall. Although many of these players, as well as Jeff Beck and even Hank Marvin, have had Signature models made for them by Fender's Custom Shop, the fact that most only differ in detail from the original Stratocaster design demonstrates the instrument's continuing appeal. According to John Mayall, perhaps the leading British evangelist for the blues in the '60s, much of the reawakening of interest in this traditional form was inspired by Stevie Ray Vaughan: 'Stevie helped revitalize the blues scene. He was a monumental figure, as important in his way in the '80s as Hendrix was in the '60s.'

Retro and Grunge | Although highly technical players such as Randy Rhoads and Eddie Van Halen were the ultimate guitar heroes at the beginning of the '80s, by the end of the decade the new heroes came from the great unwashed hordes of bands such as Guns N' Roses, The Black Crowes and Nirvana. Slash from Guns N' Roses sees himself as following a distinctly rock tradition – 'Pete Townshend, Jeff Beck and Eric

Clapton are the real heavyweights – I'm just a little peon on the rise.' When Slash abandoned his Jackson and Charvel guitars at the instigation of producer Mike Clink and took up a Les Paul he helped stimulate a long-overdue revival in Gibson's fortunes. Similarly, Slash's favourite band, The Black Crowes, represent a back-to-basics approach which combines the open tunings and sloppy chic of the Stones and Faces with old Fender and Zemaitis guitars, and resolutely old-fashioned amplifiers.

Twenty years after amplifier manufacturers introduced master volume controls to enable distortion at any volume level, guitarists are returning to the purer tone of the models which you have to crank up for distortion. As J. Mascis of Dinosaur Jr puts it, 'New amps suck bigtime!' Mascis uses older analogue pedals, old-fashioned Cry Baby wah-wahs and original '60s Fender Jazzmasters – 'They are just the coolest of guitars.' Mascis sees his music as being firmly rooted in the punk movement: 'I guess I just love loud, classic electric guitar. I hear it and it just makes me want to beat up on the guitar, any guitar. I have no interest in the blues or any of that stuff – for me classic rock starts with The Stooges. That English '70s punk thing gave me real direction.' Only a couple of years ago, his approach was unconventional – now, as companies such as Marshall and Vox re-issue their vintage designs, and guitar-makers like Charvel and Hohner introduce 'retro' guitars which evoke the feel of whacky Jazzmasters or Rickenbackers, it's a market trend, which is exacerbated as instrument manufacturers, the tabloid press and even the world's fashion houses latch on to grunge following the success of Nirvana's guitar-driven *Nevermind* album.

Forty years on from the launch of the Telecaster and Les Paul, the electric guitar's symbolism remains uniquely powerful, as a range of players, from Prince to Kurt Cobain, Nuno Bettencourt to John Lee Hooker, somehow still exploit its capacity to shock and inspire. More modern devices, such as the latest synthesizers, become outmoded and passé overnight. The electric guitar retains a timelessness of its own.

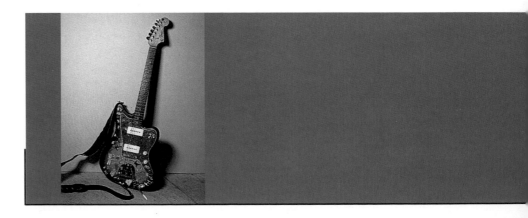

'I guess I just love loud, classic electric guitar. I hear it and it just makes me want to beat up on the guitar, any guitar' *J Mascis*

Grunge might have become fashionable with the rise of Nirvana in the early '90s (main shot: Kurt Cobain) but bands like Sonic Youth had been playing loud guitars since the mid '80s (above: Kim Gordon) Opposite left: Dinosaur Jr's J Mascis is leading a revival of the Fender Jazzmaster. This one sports his own custom paint job

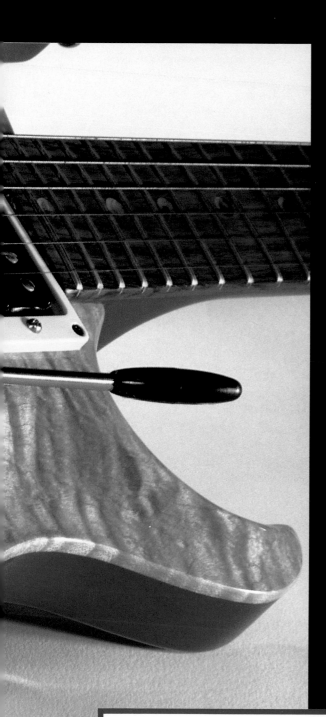

At a time when guitarists were complaining 'they don't make them like they used to,' custom guitar-maker Paul Reed Smith set out to do exactly that. The result was one of the most influential electric guitars of the '80s. At a time when other designers were concentrating on models ladened with add-ons, the PRS Custom exuded a traditional simplicity.

In his attempts to combine the looks and sound of a vintage Gibson with the practicality of a modern design, Smith has probably gone further than any other maker, with every element – from the type of glues used, to the machine head design – finely considered. The result is possibly the most highly-regarded modern production electric, but one which also demonstrates, ironically, that there is no such thing as a perfect guitar.

Paul Reed Smith Custom | 1985

State-of-the-art carved top electric guitar

Designed 1980-1982

Commercially introduced 1985

Production life 1985 to date

2

1

'Paul Reed Smith called me up and said I have a guitar I want to share with you. I'll send it to your house and if you like it we'll take it from there. I loved it straightaway. To me, the sound of guitars is like colours; with some guitars you just get green and yellow. **This guitar is like the full rainbow.'**

Carlos Santana

The main design elements of the PRS Custom are anything but original; in essence the guitar features Les Paul-type construction in a double cutaway guitar with a Strat-type tremolo, and a 25" scale length that represents a compromise between a Fender and a Gibson. This form of hybrid was one that designers had been attempting to perfect since the late '70s, but it was Smith's attention to detail that helped him succeed where his competitors had failed.

Smith started out as a custom guitar-maker in Annapolis, Maryland, and by 1980 had built up a substantial reputation as guitarists such as Carlos Santana, Peter Frampton and Neal Schon started playing his instruments. All those early guitars followed similar principles, using mahogany body/glued neck construction with a carved maple top – like a Les Paul Standard – but with a double cutaway format inspired by the Les Paul Special. Throughout this time Smith took the two types of Les Paul as a standard for the sound required, but was also working on incorporating a Strat-type tremolo. By 1985 Smith had set up a factory, attempting the ambitious task of emulating vintage models with his modern production instrument.

The production PRS followed certain principles that were well-established in the '80s, but ignored others. Significantly, Smith eschewed the use of bought-in 'vintage-style' pickups, claiming that the inherent sound of the guitar came from the woods and construction, rather than the electronics. This search for a good natural tone extended to particular discrimination in the use of timber; for his topline Artist series Smith actually auditions neck blanks for a natural 'ring' before using them. PRS guitars have always used thin lacquer finishes in order to maximize resonance, while on recent models Smith has reverted to using traditional hide glues, which he believes add extra resonance.

Although the PRS Custom's tremolo system – which was patented in 1984 – resembles that of a Strat, it was significantly reworked. The system pivots on six screws, just like the Strat, but the six screws each feature a notch into which the bridge base fits, while the whole system floats roughly 2mm above the guitar's face, making tremolo upbends far more practical than with a standard Strat trem. The tremolo block is drilled out so that the string's ball ends are much closer to the bridge saddles than on the Fender version. This minimizes the 'dead' string length, and contributes to reduced tuning problems. Other subtle improvements include stainless steel adjustment screws to avoid rust (a common problem with sweaty-handed guitarists). On a Strat tremolo these adjustment screws stand proud of the saddle, meaning it's uncomfortable to rest your hand on the bridge; on the PRS trem this fault is eliminated by a modified bridge saddle design.

The guitar's headstock retains the three-a-side layout of a Gibson, but again boasts significant differences. The nut is made from a friction-reducing nylon/teflon compound which PRS refers to as 'unobtanium'(!), while the headstock design ensures that the strings pass in a straight line from nut to machine heads; this significantly reduces friction at the nut and minimizes tuning problems with heavy tremolo usage.

Main shot: Paul Reed Smith Custom 1986
1. Body combines Les Paul Special-style shape
   with Les Paul Standard-style carved top
2. PRS tremolo models feature shallow back angle

The headstock back angle is approximately 7°, rather than the Gibson standard of 17°, again to reduce friction at the nut. Lastly, the PRS uses locking machine heads. These were a novel idea, which had been popularized by the Sperzel company, and helped improve tuning stability by reducing the amount of string wrapped around the machine head post to only a half-turn. Smith's version of this concept was an efficient one, locking the string firmly and simply.

Despite the fact that Smith maintains that pickups have a more marginal effect on a guitar's sound than is usually believed, those for the PRS are designed specifically for the instrument; on his later models Smith has attempted to emulate the sound of vintage pickups by replicating the untidy winding which was the norm when it was done by hand. Control layout is simple but effective; a single volume control features a bypass capacitor to ensure that treble is not lost at low volume settings. There is no tone control, but a five-way rotary pickup switch Is intended to emulate the versatility of the Strat system; this offers bridge humbucker alone, the two outside coils in parallel, the two inner coils in series, two inner coils in parallel and lastly neck humbucker alone. Positions 1 and 5 give typical Gibson humbucking tones, while 2, 3 and 4 give useful interpretations of a Strat's 'in between' tones. Lastly, a small 'sweet' switch offers a treble roll-off which is intended to simulate the high frequency loss of a 35' guitar lead.

Given the Paul Reed Smith's reputation, it's not surprising the guitar comes closer to emulating a vintage Gibson than most of its contemporaries. The guitar has a resonant acoustic tone that is a prerequisite of a good electric guitar, and combines the warm sustaining sound of a Les Paul with usable thinner Strat-type sounds. But in many ways the guitar has far more practical advantages than a Les Paul; the tremolo takes all but over-the-top abuse without tuning problems, but enables far quicker restringing and retuning than a Floyd-Rose system. At 8lb (3.6kg) the PRS is substantially lighter than a Les Paul, while the double cutaway design enables much easier top fret access.

As a guitar which was developed over several years, it's not surprising that the PRS Custom seems to have few practical drawbacks; it is a supremely ergonomic instrument which offers a vintage feel and a far wider combination of usable tones than many more complex instruments. Yet although Smith launched this guitar as the perfect Gibson/Fender hybrid, some of his latest models such as 1993's Dragon revert to a steeper headstock back angle, simple aluminium bridge/tailpiece, fatter neck and longer heel in search of a more authentic Les Paul tone. Although the best compromise available, the PRS Custom can't equal both the Les Paul and the Strat on their own ground. The very sophistication of the guitar also brings its own problems – it's hard to imagine a Slash or Jimmy Page outraging public decency with this sophisticated machine slung over their shoulder. But of any current production electric guitar, the PRS must be the best contender for locking up in your bank vault as a future classic.

Paul Reed Smith Custom 1985

In 1953 Gibson enhanced their credibility by producing an electric guitar in conjunction with a leading guitarist, Les Paul. Twenty-five years later, Japanese guitar company Ibanez transformed their reputation with the aid of leading guitarist Steve Vai in a similar manner. The result was a guitar that epitomized the 'superstrat' concept, and revitalized interest in artist-endorsed guitars.

Where previous Japanese guitars had simply aped their American competitors, the Ibanez Steve Vai JEM range made its rivals look staid. The JEM's technical credentials were impeccable – the guitar was playable and versatile, with an extremely effective pickup system which Vai had developed in conjunction with the American DiMarzio company. More importantly, the guitar was flash. It boasted fluorescent fittings and inlays, while one model was decorated in the same paisley material as Vai's favourite jacket. The instrument stressed frivolity and efficiency to equal degrees, and was consequently a huge success.

Ibanez Steve Vai 1987

Japanese 'player-designed' electric guitar	
Designed 1987	
Commercially introduced 1987	
Revised 1993	
Production life 1987 to date	

In the mid '80s the Ibanez name was associated with high quality but derivative instruments. The company had been making guitars since 1962, and from a variety of eccentric models changed to unashamed copies of Fender and Gibson instruments by the mid '70s. Over the next ten years the company made some effort to move from straight copies; the Artist range of 1976 was a double cutaway carved top model rather like the Yamaha SG2000, while the George Benson model of the same year was a distinctive small body electric acoustic derived from Gibson equivalents. The company had also produced Stratocaster derivatives such as the Blazer and Roadster range which attempted to develop the Stratocaster theme – with varying degrees of success. Although more successful in the American market than many other Japanese models, none of these designs changed the perception of the Ibanez name as being copyist in mentality. Parent company Hoshino set out to change this situation by recruiting guitar designer Rich Lasner to establish an American Artist Relations Centre. Within a few years Lasner had recruited endorsees of the stature of Steve Vai, Joe Satriani and Frank Gambale, incorporating their ideas into the company's production guitars.

The Artist Relations Centre's approach was devastatingly efficient. In 1986 Vai was building a reputation as sideman to Dave Lee Roth, who had left Van Halen that year. In order to gain him as endorsee, the company employed a practice which would also be repeated for Joe Satriani and Frank Gambale.

'We'd read up on what his tastes in guitars were,' says Bill Cummiskey, Department Coordinator of Hoshino US. 'We built him one of our Maxxass guitars with the pickup configuration he uses, a palm rest for the tremolo and a wild red and grey snakeskin finish. Then we sent it, all wrapped up, to his parents' house for Christmas [1986].'

Hoshino spent two anxious weeks waiting for Vai's response – when it came, his reaction was so positive that within three months he and the Hoshino team had completed a new model, designed from the ground up.

In essence the JEM range is a 'superstrat' design, derived from a standard Strat shape, with a Strat-style bolt-on neck. The guitar was optimized to suit highly technical players like Vai, who had strong ideas about guitar construction. Hence the body was made out of a light but resonant American basswood, the guitar used a switching arrangement Vai had developed with American pickup company DiMarzio, and, just as importantly, the instrument

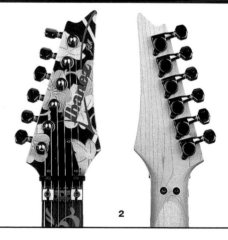

Main shot: The model pictured is the Steve Vai JEM 77; it features Vai's favourite fabric sealed under the polyester finish!
1&2. A Floyd Rose-style string lock is attached by two bolts through the neck. The spliced headstock joint is just visible at the bottom of pic 2
3. Floyd Rose-derived tremolo is fitted in 'lion's claw' recess

1   2

sported distinctive visual features such as a 'monkeygrip' cut into the guitar's upper bout, and fluorescent fret markers and pickups.

The JEM employs a body shape based on the crudely modified Charvel guitars Vai had used previously, derived from Fender's Stratocaster but with both horns lengthened, and both cutaways extending more deeply into the body. Together with a cutaway heel neck joint, this significantly eased access to the neck, which retained the familiar 25$^{1}/_{2}$" Fender scale length, but featured 24 frets – the top four scalloped, to allow a guitarist to 'dig in'.

The JEM utilized the Ibanez 'Edge' tremolo, a development of the industry standard Floyd Rose system. The Ibanez version featured improvements like stud lock posts and a push-in arm which would stay in position, rather than flop out of reach like that of a Strat. The body features a 'lion's claw' recess behind the trem; this allows upwards bends without the fine tuners jamming against the body, while the tuners themselves sit further back, allowing guitarists to rest their right hand comfortably in the bridge. The Ibanez locking nut is again similar to the Floyd Rose original.

Ibanez necks helped standardize a shallow profile which is now common in superstrats; but their characteristic shape was only used on the RG range – the JEM featured a slightly fatter neck as favoured by Vai – 19mm in depth at the nut. The tilted back headstock is made from a separate piece of maple spliced on to the neck, a typical arrangement for Ibanez electric guitars.

Pickups were acknowledged as a weak point in Japanese guitars of the '70s and '80s; Ibanez tackled this problem by developing pickups in association with DiMarzio. The system developed for Vai was basically conventional, featuring humbucking neck and bridge pickups, but a single-coil middle pickup. All pickups are bolted directly to the guitar's body; some guitarists feel this gives a more resonant sound. A five-way switch enables selection of each pickup separately, but in positions 2 and 4 gives the middle pickup with the inside coils of the neck or bridge humbucker respectively. This meant that positions 2, 3 and 4 enabled traditional Strat sounds, while 1 and 5 gave the higher output of the humbucking pickups.

Lastly, the Ibanez Steve Vai model was visually distinctive; the fashion in heavy rock guitars of the time was for Satanist imagery, dark finishes and skull insignia; Vai dictated a reaction against this in the form of fluorescent touches on the three models; on the JEM 77 pickup and control knobs were

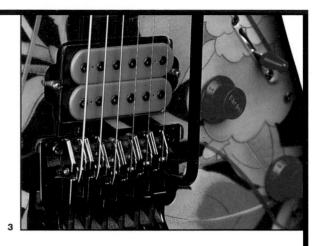

3

in fluorescent pink plastics, while the flat rosewood fingerboard featured fluorescent green 'vine' markers.

Although easily categorized as a 'metal' instrument, the JEM 77 is surprisingly versatile. The humbucking pickups are more powerful than the equivalent Strat positions, but are voiced to simulate a Gibson PAF, rather than a high output type; this avoids the thin, nasal sound which often afflicts superstrats. 'Inbetween' positions, on the other hand, possess most of the snap and life of the Strat equivalent. At approximately 8lb (3.6kg) in weight the guitar is as manageable as a typical Strat, while the 'monkeygrip', ostensibly a gimmick, is actually a handy way of carrying the guitar off its strap.

Five months after Hoshino sent Vai a 'Christmas' guitar, the company had completed the first production samples of the new model in Japan. The JEM guitar, and the RG range – a lower-priced derivative – were launched at the NAMM industry trade show in June to instant acclaim. Cummiskey admits the company were initially sceptical about the instrument's fluorescent regalia, 'but the timing was right – people were ready for a change – and the fact that it looked striking and had genuinely new technical features like the lion's claw recess caused a lot of excitement'. The Steve Vai model was expensive but aspirational, and helped the Ibanez company carve out a distinctive niche; it also revived the concept of the artist-designed guitar; both Fender and Washburn would increase the profile of their Artist Relations operation in the wake of Ibanez's success, while Japanese rivals Yamaha poached Lasner to head their own R&D team. The development process behind the JEM, if not the guitar itself, has left an indelible mark on guitar design.

'Right now I don't want to play anything but the Ibanez. They've just perfected that guitar for me – **the sound, the look, the feel** – and live it sounds **great**' *Steve Vai*

Ibanez Steve Vai 1987

Fifty years on from the birth of the Telecaster and Les Paul, it seems that these classic guitars still overawe today's designers. Ken Parker is one of the few to escape from their spell. The Parker Artist looks radical, yet most of its innovation isn't apparent at first sight. The antithesis of its Fender and Gibson forebears, whose solid bodies were intended to minimize resonance, the Artist glories in its spruce body, which renders it a space-age cousin to the centuries-old acoustic guitar.

Ken Parker's first electrics took what seemed like an age to come off the production line and its futuristic looks and high price mean mass-market acceptance is unlikely. Yet against the odds, Parker has demonstrated that the development of the electric guitar has not reached a dead end.

Parker Artist | 1997

Lightweight 'extra resonant' electric guitar

Designed 1991-1997

Commercially introduced 1997

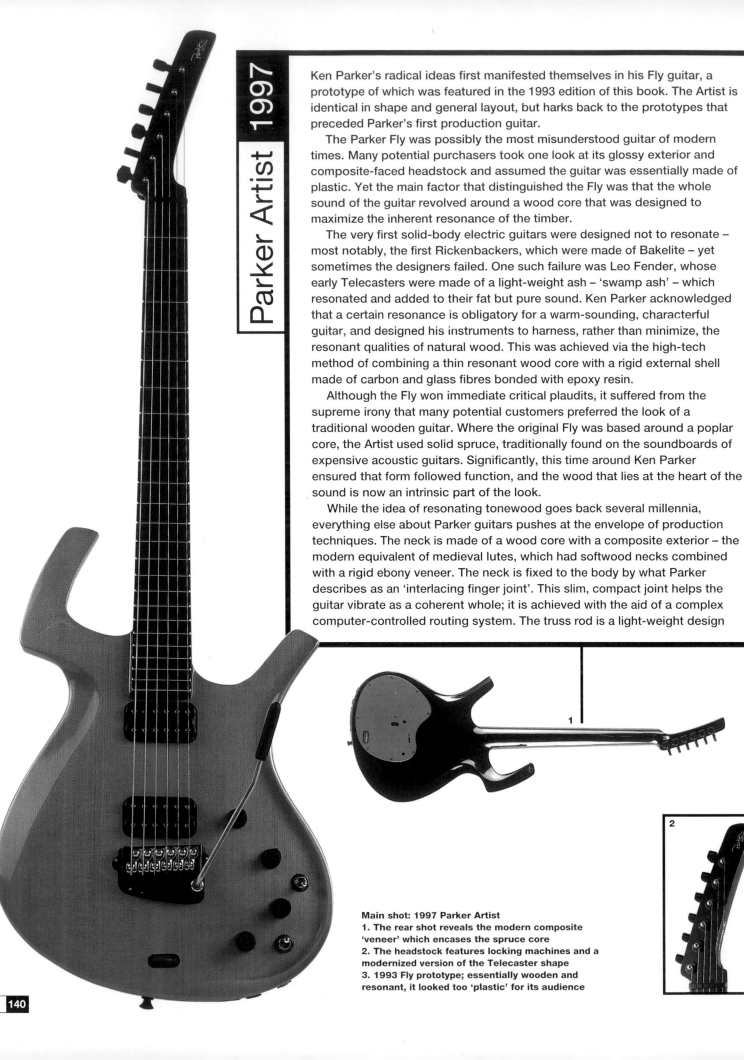

Ken Parker's radical ideas first manifested themselves in his Fly guitar, a prototype of which was featured in the 1993 edition of this book. The Artist is identical in shape and general layout, but harks back to the prototypes that preceded Parker's first production guitar.

The Parker Fly was possibly the most misunderstood guitar of modern times. Many potential purchasers took one look at its glossy exterior and composite-faced headstock and assumed the guitar was essentially made of plastic. Yet the main factor that distinguished the Fly was that the whole sound of the guitar revolved around a wood core that was designed to maximize the inherent resonance of the timber.

The very first solid-body electric guitars were designed not to resonate – most notably, the first Rickenbackers, which were made of Bakelite – yet sometimes the designers failed. One such failure was Leo Fender, whose early Telecasters were made of a light-weight ash – 'swamp ash' – which resonated and added to their fat but pure sound. Ken Parker acknowledged that a certain resonance is obligatory for a warm-sounding, characterful guitar, and designed his instruments to harness, rather than minimize, the resonant qualities of natural wood. This was achieved via the high-tech method of combining a thin resonant wood core with a rigid external shell made of carbon and glass fibres bonded with epoxy resin.

Although the Fly won immediate critical plaudits, it suffered from the supreme irony that many potential customers preferred the look of a traditional wooden guitar. Where the original Fly was based around a poplar core, the Artist used solid spruce, traditionally found on the soundboards of expensive acoustic guitars. Significantly, this time around Ken Parker ensured that form followed function, and the wood that lies at the heart of the sound is now an intrinsic part of the look.

While the idea of resonating tonewood goes back several millennia, everything else about Parker guitars pushes at the envelope of production techniques. The neck is made of a wood core with a composite exterior – the modern equivalent of medieval lutes, which had softwood necks combined with a rigid ebony veneer. The neck is fixed to the body by what Parker describes as an 'interlacing finger joint'. This slim, compact joint helps the guitar vibrate as a coherent whole; it is achieved with the aid of a complex computer-controlled routing system. The truss rod is a light-weight design

Main shot: 1997 Parker Artist
1. The rear shot reveals the modern composite 'veneer' which encases the spruce core
2. The headstock features locking machines and a modernized version of the Telecaster shape
3. 1993 Fly prototype; essentially wooden and resonant, it looked too 'plastic' for its audience

which is adjusted simply at the headstock end, while the stainless steel frets are positioned directly onto the phenolic fingerboard.

The Artist's two conventional magnetic humbucking pickups, designed by Larry Blucher of DiMarzio, are combined with six piezo-electronic pickups, designed by Larry Fishman, located within the bridge saddles, which provide a more 'acoustic' tone.

The Parker's vibrato design is derived from that of a Strat, combined with a friction-reducing nut and locking machine heads. The vibrato unit itself is made of lightweight alloy, with saddle heights matched to the fingerboard camber – this reduces the number of moving parts, allowing optimum transmission of acoustic energy. The vibrato unit uses a flat spring – essential with a guitar this thin – which is more consistent than traditional springs. A simple sliding 'step-stop switch' disables the vibrato, while the knurled 'balance wheel' controls the tension of the spring plate, allowing the vibrato to be set for regular up/down, down-only, or fixed position use – a degree of control unthinkable to most Stratocaster users...

The Parker's high tech design gives the guitarist a huge range of options, but the basic sound gets right to the resonant, almost acoustic-like tone of the classic '50s solidbodies. Turn down an old Les Paul, Strat or Tele and they can sound almost acoustic; turn them up and they scream with balanced highs and lows. The Artist approaches that feel, but augments it with a modern electro-acoustic tone from the piezo pickups. Mixed with the magnetic pickups, they give an almost unlimited range of options.

Nearly a decade on from those first prototypes, Parker guitars still remain a rarefied taste. The electric guitar industry, now over 50 years old, is a conservative marketplace and the Parker's hefty price tag presents its own problems, despite the fact that accounting for inflation it comes pretty close to the $189 launch price of Leo Fender's Telecaster. The guitar has still won acceptance from high-tech musicians like Reeves Gabrels, as well as gospel – and Stratocaster – pioneer Pops Staples.

At a time when heritage becomes more and more pervasive – and even oppressive – the Parker Artist shows it's still possible to redesign the electric guitar from first principles and come up with a genuinely superior design – and one that boasts many of the qualities that made its half-century old forebears so highly prized.

"What Ken Parker invented was a truly radical instrument, so ergonomic and familiar that any Strat player could close their eyes and feel at home. Like Leo Fender before him, the guitar and tremolo system was

new, visionary and unbelievably practical.

The bridge alone is an amazing combination of the voluptuous and the functional, with a sonic quality that equals or surpasses that holy grail, the vintage Strat trem. Beyond that, the guitar has a piezo system that is sweeter than any bridge transducer.

For all these reasons and more I feel Ken Parker is the only guitar designer and builder whose name can be mentioned in the same breath as Leo Fender. And like Leo, he is ahead of his time."

Reeves Gabrels

3

Diverse decades

The beginning of the 21st century marked a significant staging post in the history of the electric guitar: suddenly all the iconic solid body guitars – the Telecaster, Les Paul and Stratocaster – were approaching their 50th birthdays. Since its space-age, futuristic first appearance, it could be argued that the electric guitar has hardly changed. Those three icons still remain – in reverse order – the most popular electric guitars on the planet, whether they come from Fender or Gibson, the company's own licensed brands like Squier (Fender) Epiphone (Gibson), or the numerous lookalike brands that continue to flourish. Yet the last decade of the 20th century was one of the instrument's most colourful. As ever, the reasons behind the stylistic trends that emerged were nearly as diverse as the instruments themselves. But the primary influence on guitar design, in the '90s and beyond, was that of the musicians who used the instrument.

The Legacy of Grunge Even as grunge took up permanent residence in the charts, guitar shops were apparently still stocked with the pointy-headed, widdle-rock guitars that had dominated the '80s. The new players favoured the classic – and in many cases, out-of-favour – likes of Fender's Jaguar and Jazzmaster, the Les Paul Deluxe, Junior and Special, not to mention the SG. Although sales of used guitars soared, the musical instrument industry was ill-prepared for this turnaround.

The Brit-pop explosion of the mid-'90s may not have spread to the US, but bands like Oasis – and reinvigorated heroes such as Paul Weller – again helped promote classic yet neglected instruments, such as Epiphone's Riviera and Casino. As guitar gods like Steve Vai and Joe Satriani, together with larger, established rock bands, found their sales dropping, so did the instrument companies that had supported them. If they didn't have a classic, proven design to reissue then they would have to invent one.

Ironically Charvel – responsible for the now-derided pointy head rock axes – was one of the first companies to reinvent its own history, providing the first significant example of retro guitar design, in which old design motifs are re-arranged or used as inspiration for a new model that looks pleasantly familiar. The company's

Main photo: Noel Gallagher of Oasis signals a revival of the semi-acoustic.
New, but familiar: Gretsch SilverJet, DeArmond Starfire, Fender Cyclone, Danelectro 56-U2 and Charvel Surfcaster

Surfcaster, which combined lipstick tube pickups with a semi-solid body bolt-on neck design that recalled the Jazzmaster and Telecaster Thinline, was introduced in 1991 and was soon taken up by bands such as the UK's influential My Bloody Valentine. Suddenly, kitsch appeal took over from ergonomics, as 'antiquated' designs – noticeably the Bigsby vibrato – returned, repackaged with gaudy sparkle paintwork and 'mother-of-toilet-seat' pearloid. In 1992 Ibanez tried via a sister brand, Starfield, to augment its flagging rock-guitar catalogue with original retro designs. Under its own name, the Talman trod a similar path.

In reality, few retro designs had lasting impact. Fender entered the fray in 1997 with the short-lived Squier Vista series. Courtney Love was one of the designers for the new but retro range, contributing the Venus 6- and 12-string, but the more sensible Jagmaster, with two humbuckers, reflected a common enough modification of Fender's Jazzmaster.

Although Epiphone enjoyed great success with a cost-effective version of its own classics, and those of its sister company, Gibson, Fender's attempt to capture some of that market via the DeArmond by Guild line failed to make as much impact. Introduced in 1998, the brand was dropped without any announcement in 2001. It would seem that the Guild solids and semis on which the line was based were no match for the Gibson designs so popular in Epiphone's line. Fender's own-brand late-'90s retro efforts were more successful: the Cyclone, which used Mustang references but with a bridge humbucker, and the twin humbucking Toronado remained in the line in 2001.

Reissue or die Although some companies' attempts at fictionalized 'reissues' met with failure, those with genuine heritage to revisit often prospered. Danelectro is one of the most visible examples. The company's re-emergence in 1997, with a funky line of retro-inspired effect pedals, paved the way for guitars the following year. Initially it was the twin pickup '56-U2, a close copy of the original model, followed by further reissues and new, highly retro designs that retained the old Danelectro ethos. The obvious success of the line, however, probably derives as much from sound business sense as from the funky tone and feel of these bargain basement instruments. The initial guitars were affordable enough to appeal to a new generation, not to mention to those players who remembered Danos from the first time around. Combine that with excellent worldwide marketing and intelligent designs and it's no surprise that this venture was one of the successes of the '90s.

Historically, Gretsch had a huge seam to mine when the brand reappeared in 1989 with Japanese-made models; the brand's contribution to music was so significant that its return was more significant than a mere vagary of fashion. Although most of the new Gretsch designs were reissues, the company used signature models to update its appeal, from Duane Eddy, Brian Setzer and the less-obvious, but highly respected, Bryan Adams side-man Keith Scott, not to mention AC/DC's Malcolm Young. By the turn of the century, Gretsch had developed the more affordable Korean-made Historic and even lower-priced Electromatic ranges.

In 1991, Burns of London introduced authentic reissues of the groundbreaking British guitars. Quirky-looking, but ergonomically well thought-out, they were used by several high profile new British faces, such as Gaz Coombes of Supergrass. Burns introduced its own Korean-made guitar, the Club Series Marquee, in 1999. But it wasn't just designs from the pioneering days of the electric guitar that returned to the stores. For example, Ampeg, Dean, Yamaha, and Ibanez all reissued models from their archives.

Business matters

Compared to the early days of the electric guitar, obvious innovation in the '90s seemed thin on the ground. The Parker Fly, introduced in 1994, remains a beacon of innovation. Its radical outline presented inevitable difficulties. However, the piezo-loaded bridge technology which the Fly popularized did launch its own trend. As the decade progressed and retro-fit piezo-loaded bridges like Fishman's Powerbridge became readily available, so more and more companies offered 'hybrid' guitars, which combined standard electric and new 'acoustic' tones.

Much of the innovation of the '90s has taken place on the production line, rather than in the design process. The trend to overseas manufacturing, concentrated notably in Japan, Korea, Taiwan and China, didn't always produce the best-made guitars; but it did produce affordable ones. However, just as manufacturing in Japan became less feasible due to rising domestic costs and economic recession, Korea, too, encountered problems. With the reduced demand for electric guitars, this meant many of the larger Far Eastern factories had to down-size. However, this uncertainty was in some respects beneficial, as many American companies invested in computer-aided production: design, wood-shaping, inlaying, finishing and buffing. Production efficiency assumed a new importance. Fender, for example, not only moved to a new state-of-the-art facility in Corona, but also removed the need for Japanese-made Fender product by investing in a Mexican plant in Ensenada. Along the way, the Fender Custom Shop – also in Corona – became, in terms of output, around the sixth largest guitar company in the USA.

But despite these production-efficient strategies, even the smaller companies like PRS, Parker and Music Man began, by the turn of the century, to offer Far Eastern product way below the price of their USA-made guitars. Parker's P-38 and PRS's Santana SE are fine examples of Korean-made guitars and are much more than mere copies of their USA line. In both cases the companies were able to take advantage of the Korean guitar industry's desire, in the wake of their own declining output, to offer quality over – relatively speaking – quantity.

Mainstream Moves

But what of the two electric guitar giants: Fender and Gibson? Clearly the return to classic designs benefited both, and both companies capitalized on their heritage. Just as well, as original new models were thin on the ground. Gibson's M-III Series electrics of 1991 just didn't live up to the name on the headstock. 1993's Nighthawk fared better, while the later single-coil Blueshawk brought back some of the elegant simplicity crucial to a classic Gibson design.

Although Gibson's custom shop dates back to the '60s, a new venture was launched in 1992. Like the Fender Custom Shop, it was essentially a separate company from the main production-line concern. Apart from limited edition, profile-raising one-offs, there were plenty of new designs. Alongside semi-hollow Les Pauls and down-sized ES335s, the Gibson Custom, Art & Historic Division – as the custom shop was grandly named – created the DC Pro in 1997. This model inspired 1998's production-line DC Studio and Standard before those two models merged into the Studio Standard Lite and then the Standard Double Cut Plus in 2001. These guitars combined the double cutaway outline of the post-1958 Les Paul Special with the arched top of the standard Les Paul – the blend Paul Reed Smith had used way back in the early '80s.

Gibson DC Studio, Music Man John Petrucci, PRS Santana SE and Fender Relic Tele.

Gaz Coombes of Supergrass: helped spearhead a revival of the long-dormant Burns guitar.

But for all the experimentation, Gibson, like Fender, primarily used its Custom Shop to offer high-spec versions of their respective classics. In the mid-90s, Fender experimented with their 'Relic' concept: an aged-looking new guitar. Reputedly Keith Richards received some Custom Shop models for a Rolling Stones tour and told the Custom Shop 'bash 'em up a bit and I'll play 'em.' Fender was surprised by the interest, but by 1999 the Relic concept formed the major part of the Custom Shop's output. Subsequently, Gibson too offered 'aged' Les Pauls and SGs.

Yet it is Fender who seem to have steered the straightest course into the new millennium. Along with production changes – for the better – Fender's product line was constantly rationalized on all levels. In 1999 Fender Mexico began their Classic series, which replaced the popular Japanese-built reissues. In their USA line the long-lived American Standard Series was re-worked with better timber specification and detail changes into the American Series. The American Deluxe series added more bells and whistles, like noise-cancelling single-coil pickups, while the American Vintage series bridged the price gap between the more affordable Classic series and the more expensive Custom Shop Relics.

New Challengers

The return to tone, as some have put it, also benefited quality-led brands like PRS and the Ernie Ball-owned Music Man. More than one observer has referred to PRS as the new Gibson and Music Man as the new Fender. Both companies are run by charismatic figures: Paul Reed Smith and Sterling Ball (Ernie's son) who – unlike Leo Fender and Gibson's Ted McCarty – are both pro-level musicians.

The early '90s was a period of change for PRS, as Smith began to believe he could improve the core tone of his guitars by producing a stiffer, shorter neck and one-piece wrapover bridge and re-voicing his pickups. First introduced on the limited edition Dragon guitar, these features were incorporated into the Custom line in 1993 as the PRS Custom 22. In 1994, Smith honoured the input and influence of Gibson's Ted McCarty by producing the McCarty Model – which got closer still to that '50s Gibson vibe and tone.

As the '90s progressed PRS produced further 'new classic' guitars, from the Santana model through the innovative hollow-bodied Hollowbody to, at the start of the new millennium, the Single-Cut – Smith's take on Gibson's finest. With quality and production on the up, PRS moved into numerous stylistic camps and many of the new bands, like Limp Bizkit and Creed, not to mention plenty of the old school, were playing PRS by the end of the decade.

Music Man's success took longer to establish; while their 1986 Silhouette design brought them credibility thanks to Keith Richards, it was the Eddie Van Halen

signature model that put them on the map. Although Music Man's signature range features some of the finest players in the world – Albert Lee, Steve Morse, Steve Lukather and John Petrucci – it's the quality, feel and tone of the production models that continues to impress, as the company turns out custom shop quality at production line prices.

Sign your name

In a decade that supposedly lacked guitar heroes there has been no shortage of signature guitars. Eddie Van Halen designed his Music Man guitar in conjunction with Dudley Gimpel and Stirling Ball. It appeared in 1991, combining a worn-in feel neck, with a flat, maple-fronted basswood body, two custom-wound DiMarzio humbuckers and the ubiquitous Floyd Rose vibrato. By 1996 Eddie had changed his allegiance to the Peavey company with the much-hyped EVH Wolfgang. But Peavey's guitar-making reputation didn't match that of Music Man, who renamed Eddie's guitar the Axis and used it as the basis of a successful new range.

The new guitar 'gods' – like Kurt Cobain –initially ran shy of product endorsement. Later, however, Cobain commissioned the Fender Custom Shop to build him his Jag-stang, conceived by centrally slicing pictures of a Fender Jaguar and Mustang and sticking them back together. Fender produced a posthumous Japanese-made version, which didn't prove anywhere near as popular or influential as the man's music.

As Brit-pop accounted for the sales of countless semi-acoustic guitars, the movement's crown prince, Noel Gallagher, was lured into the signature stakes with his Epiphone Supernova, basically a Riviera with stud tailpiece and, of course, in sky blue, Manchester City soccer club's colours.

PRS too would thank their lucky bird inlays for Carlos Santana. Longtime PRS fan Carlos revived a flagging career with the massive-selling *Supernatural*. Shortly before, in 1995, PRS had started production of the high-end Santana model; by 2001 they had a standard-priced version and the Korean-made Santana SE.

Whereas at one time a big signature artist would ensure massive sales, the signature guitars of the '90s and beyond are more niche affairs. The UK's Guitarist magazine listed over 100 signature models available in August 2001 – where Korn's Head and Munky 7-strings sit aside commemorative models dedicated to players like Muddy Waters, John Lee Hooker and John Lennon.

Danelectro DC3 1999

The term 'retro design' might be seen as a disparaging one, but it's one that's made its way into the mass market, with the appearance of 'modern' versions of vintage automobiles such as the Mini, the VW Beetle and Nissan's cutesie-pie Figaro. Danelectro, a 1947 company resurrected for the 1990s, followed a similar path with this updated rendition of a legendary American budget guitar, resurrected in a Korean-made version. Uniquely, however, the DC3 retains everything that made the original Danelectros inefficient, unique, delectable – and the epitome of cheap'n'cheerful.

The first Danelectros were designed as bargain-basement mail order instruments for the Sears, Roebuck company. They had two main quirks: the guitars were made of 'Masonite' – a forerunner of what we'd today call hardboard – and the unique 'lipstick pickups' were, as the name suggested, cased in surplus chromed tubes from a lipstick manufacturer. Those quirks ensured that Danelectro guitars looked and sounded like nothing else on the market. Nearly 50 years on, that's still the case.

| Updated variant of 1958 budget electric |
| Designed 1999 |
| Commercially introduced 1999 |
| Production life 1999 to date |
| |
| |

Nat Daniel, who set up his company in 1947, was as original a thinker as Leo Fender or Ken Parker; his ideas, however, weren't quite as sophisticated. Danelectro guitars were above all cheap and to make them at such a low cost required some real innovation. The prime example of this was the body construction. Masonite had been developed around 1924 by William Mason, who invented this cheap wood substitute by accident after attempting to make a thermal insulation material from compressed wood dust and glue. Danelectro guitars used two thick Masonite panels as the front and back of the guitar, sandwiching a semi-solid poplar core. This method of construction bore a passing resemblance to that of early Gretsch semi-solid guitars, except that most people would describe a Danelectro as being more 'semi' than 'solid.' The neck construction, too, was unconventional; the wood used was poplar, with an aluminium tube providing reinforcement in place of the more commonplace adjustable truss rod.

The lipstick tubes used as pickup covers dispensed with the need for any expensive pressing or machining; the coils of wire and magnets were arranged to fit the casing, rather than vice versa. The same approach of using existing, low-priced components extended to the pickup switch, which reportedly was originally destined for lighting circuits. When used to select both pickups at once, this switch wired them in series rather than the customary parallel arrangement; both pickups together hence sounded much louder than either pickup by itself – an impractical, but once again distinctive arrangement.

Finally, the bridge design too was unique; a chromed plate was adjusted in height via three screws, and the strings passed over a simple rosewood saddle, rather like the ivory version found on many acoustic guitars.

Although Danelectro guitars were produced in large numbers, particularly the Silvertone-badged models made for Sears, Roebuck, by 1967 Nat Daniel had sold the business and production at the New Jersey factory was soon terminated. The company gained a brief new lease of life via New York retailer Dan Armstrong, who produced superior guitars made from

Danelectro DC3 1999

'I have one expensive guitar I love, a 1936 Martin acoustic. But when you're using a **load of effects pedals, there's nothing better than a cheap guitar!"**

Beck

Main shot: The DC3 is based on the company's 1958 'shorthorn' Deluxe with updated hardware.
1. The shape and construction of the body is faithful to original Danelectros, but the neck design and improved machineheads show its modern origins
2. The redesigned bridge improves on the single rosewood saddle of the original guitars, with six adjustable saddles for improved intonation

2

Danelectro parts up to 1970 before launching his own range of guitars.

Nearly three decades later, as vintage Fenders and Gibsons became prohibitively expensive, original Danelectros became relatively collectible. In 1997 the Evets Corporation purchased the brand name and launched a series of effects pedals; an electric guitar range, based around reasonably faithful, Korean-made versions of the company's best-known guitars, followed shortly thereafter. The DC3, a new design based on early Danelectro 'shorthorn' guitars, appeared in 1999.

Where many 'retro' design ape the look, but not the construction, of their forebears, the DC-3 is remarkably faithful to the guitars that inspired it. Most significantly, the Masonite front panels are combined with a semi-solid core – of plywood, rather than poplar. Unusual when these guitars first appeared, this construction is drastically unconventional by present-day standards, when most electric guitars are simple variants of Fender or Gibson designs. The neck design is, in contrast, conventional: a maple construction, with a standard adjustable truss rod. An updated version of the Danelectro circuitry features three pickups which can be combined in pairs; a simple toggle switch connects all three at once. As with the original, the pickups are combined in series, rather than in parallel.

The recreated Danelectro boasts several ergonomic improvements over its forebears; its intonation can be set more accurately, the modern machineheads are far more efficient and the truss rod is more practical than the original. Yet these improvements are hardly the point. The DC3 is still impractical – different pickup selections can vary wildly in volume, the body construction causes problems with microphony – but the very roughness of the sound evokes a long-lost era. Clanky and abrasive in single-pickup mode, chunky and heavy with two pickups combined, it's perfectly suited to an era when musicians are searching out primitive, roots inspirations.

Most 'retro' design is simply a matter of cosmetics – for instance, the new Volkswagen Beetle, which apes the look but features none of the distinctive design features of its ancestor. The Danelectro DC3, which has no claims to practicality or versatility, would probably have no claim to classic status were it not for the fact that, unlike the new VW Beetle, it retains the most crucial feature of its forebear: its ludicrously affordable price tag.

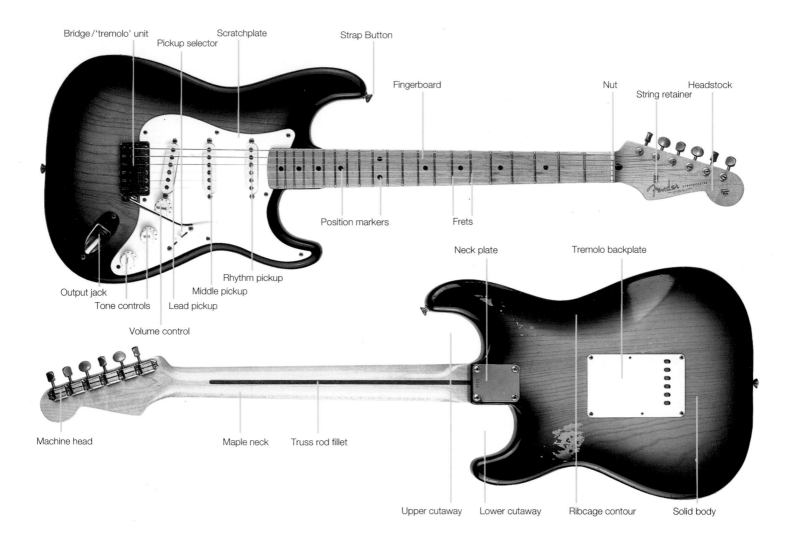

Bridge/'tremolo' unit
Pickup selector
Scratchplate
Strap Button
Fingerboard
Nut
Headstock
String retainer
Position markers
Frets
Neck plate
Tremolo backplate
Rhythm pickup
Output jack
Middle pickup
Tone controls
Lead pickup
Volume control
Machine head
Maple neck
Truss rod fillet
Upper cutaway
Lower cutaway
Ribcage contour
Solid body

The basic elements of a solid body guitar such as the Stratocaster shown above are simple, but seemingly slight variations in construction of materials of each element can substantially affect the tone of the instrument.

A guitar's inherent sound comes from the interaction of all of its elements; thus attributing the distinctive sound of a Gibson electric to the use of humbucking pickups alone, for example, would be nonsensical. Although one of the design aims for solid body electric guitars was to eliminate body vibrations, or resonances, electric guitars do resonate; that is what gives a guitar its distinctive sound. Play a Gibson Les Paul

acoustically, and then a Telecaster, and you'll find they sound very different. A solid body guitar forms a whole resonant structure; the various elements of this structure, such as the body, neck, headstock or pickups all have their own resonant peaks and troughs. Some of the sonic differences between Fenders and Gibsons can be explained quite easily; others are more problematic. We know that single coil pickups contribute to a Fender's bright sound, but how much difference does the headstock design make, for instance? It's difficult (and often meaningless) to isolate the particular from the general.

Sometimes it appears that the wondrous sound of classic guitars arrived almost by chance: Leo Fender, for example, decided to use a bolt-on maple neck for the Telecaster because it simplified repair and construction, and because maple was readily available, as was the ash used for the body. The resulting bright sound perfectly suited the Country musicians Leo was trying to capture. All classic inventions have had their share of happy accidents.

Body Material | The common woods used in guitar bodies are mahogany, alder, ash, maple and – on more recent guitars – basswood and poplar. Gibson solid bodies have traditionally favoured mahogany construction, while most Fender bodies are made of ash or alder.

It is often simplistic to generalize about the 'sound' of particular woods: the term mahogany, for example, covers a huge amount of different timbers, while the condition (ie dryness and seasoning) of timber crucially affects the resonance and stability of an electric guitar.

However, there are general parameters. Gibson's use of mahogany is one contributor to what is generally considered to be a rounder, fatter sound. As Jol Dantzig, previously director of design at the US makers Hamer, explains: 'On a superficial level you could say the harder the wood, the brighter the tone. But this explanation is misleading because extremely light-weight wood is bright, for different reasons.' According to Dantzig, dense, hard woods like ebony or rock maple produce a brilliant sound – 'the vibration isn't absorbed by the wood, and simply bounces off it.' Medium density woods like alder and mahogany give a warmer and bassier tone, while lighter woods which vibrate more easily, such as the American 'swamp ash' used on some early Telecasters, give a brighter, papery, more 'acoustic' sound. Combinations of woods will obviously interact, such as the example of the Gibson Les Paul which has a maple cap to add brightness on top of a mahogany slab (according to Ted McCarty, Gibson tried making all-maple prototypes, but these were very heavy).

1. Ibanez JEM with basswood body
2. Fender Stratocaster with ash body
3. Gibson Les Paul Standard; 'red'-coloured wood is mahogany; contoured top is maple

1. Gretsch White Falcon: acoustic electric (or hollow body)
2. Music Man Silhouette: solid body
3. Gibson ES335: semi-acoustic (or semi-solid)

Body Classification | The current convention for classifying electric guitars is to split them into three types. Electric guitars such as the Gibson ES150, which have hollow, generally arch-top, bodies and have a magnetic pickup fitted are termed 'electric acoustics', or 'hollow body electrics' (US). The Gibson ES335, which has a hollow body with a solid central sustain block, was the first example of a 'semi-acoustic' or 'semi-hollow' (US). The ES335 is also referred to as 'semi-solid'; this term also applies to guitars such as the Fender Tele Thinline which have acoustic chambers carved out of an essentially solid body. The Gibson Les Paul and Fender Telecaster are solid body electrics.

In addition, guitars such as the Washburn Festival series, which are intended to provide an accurate amplified acoustic tone, are termed 'electro-acoustics' or, confusingly, electric/ acoustics – Ovation, who pioneered this concept, call their guitars 'acoustic electrics'.

It's easy to get into semantics here. Many would refer to a Gretsch Chet Atkins 6120 as a 'semi-acoustic' even though it doesn't have that central sustain block – this area is rendered more confusing by the fact that apparently similar guitars such as the ES335 and ES330 are, respectively, semi-acoustic and hollow body guitars (they can both be referred to as 'thinline electrics').

Necks | Most electric guitar necks are made of mahogany or maple. The key requirement for a guitar neck is stiffness; if the neck vibrates, energy is lost, damaging sustain, while very flexible necks cause unstable tuning. Lately manufacturers such as Paul Reed Smith have returned to fatter necks in the search for the ultimate tone.

Where Gibson traditionally use mahogany for their necks, Fender use rock maple, which contributes to their guitars' hard, clear sound. Laminate necks, which use several strips of wood, have been used by many companies including Gibson (who introduced laminated necks in 1969), Zemaitis, and Hamer. Laminated construction can help increase the stability of the neck, and renders the quality and conditioning of timber arguably less crucial, enabling more consistency in a mass production environment.

Composite necks have proved most popular in the bass guitar field, primarily to eliminate the problem of dead spots, where the resonant frequency of the guitar coincides with a note on the fingerboard, cancelling some of the string's energy. Although moulded graphite/epoxy composites have been used by the likes of Modulus, Status and Steinberger, current thinking tends towards using graphite rods within a wooden neck, to provide added stiffness but retain the tonal qualities of wood.

The adjustable truss rod, invented by Gibson's Thaddeus McHugh in 1922 to stop necks warping under string tension, now primarily serves to allow specific adjustment of the 'bow' or relief of a neck. Early designs only counteracted string tension, whereas modern dual action designs provide more flexible adjustment with the use of lighter gauge strings. Truss rod adjustment should be straightforward, but often isn't. Many Fenders require removal of a guitar's scratchplate; the company improved on this method with the 'bullet' truss rod adjustment of the late '60s. Unfortunately, this efficient system has become damned by its association with a fall in Fender production standards at that time.

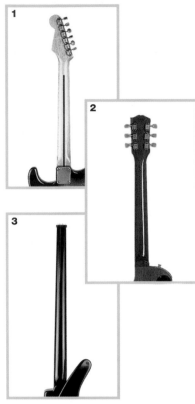

1: Maple Strat neck with truss rod inserted from back; note 'skunk stripe'
2. Mahogany Les Paul neck
3. Graphite/epoxy composite Steinberger neck

1. One piece maple Strat neck, 7.25" fretboard radius
2. Rosewood Les Paul fretboard, 12" radius
3. Ebony Jackson Soloist fretboard, conical radius
4. Rosewood PRS fretboard, 10" radius

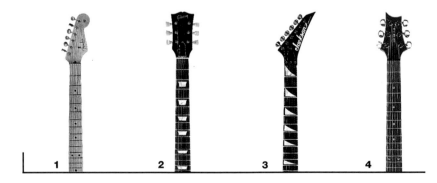

Fingerboards | The construction of a guitar's fingerboard affects both sound and playability.

Early Fender guitars used a one-piece maple neck. This 'stiff' wood enhances the upper harmonic content, and is generally thought to make these guitars sound snappier and funkier.

Ebony, for fingerboard use, also emphasises the treble content of a guitar's sound – it's very dense and can actually contribute to the stiffness of the neck. Rosewood is less dense than maple or ebony; some players find it sounds 'bigger' and smoother. The extent to which the sound will vary depends on the thickness of the fingerboard (some Fender rosewood fingerboards are very thin, almost a veneer) while many guitarists feel that there's a definite sonic difference between one-piece maple necks, and the late '60s type, as used by Jimi Hendrix, which had a glued-on maple fingerboard.

Fingerboard camber significantly affects the feel of the neck. Gibson guitars have traditionally used a flatter camber, of 12" radius. Early Fenders have a much more extreme camber, of 7 1/4" radius. This was introduced for comfort, but with the advent of string bending can cause 'choking' when playing high up the fingerboard. Some modern guitars solve this problem with a compound radius, which means the fretboard will be flatter high up the neck, but will have a more extreme camber (smaller radius) near the nut. PRS and Music Man use a compromise 10" radius.

Frets | Gibson have traditionally used 22-fret necks, while Fender have featured 21. Danelectro have made a guitar which featured 36! Simply speaking, more frets give you more notes, which are useful if you like playing high up the fingerboard, particularly for tapping – or if you're a show off. Many Fender-style guitars now feature 24 frets, but adding more frets can compromise the position of the rhythm pickup. Fret size and shape also substantially affect the feel of a guitar from a player's point of view, and width of common types varies widely, from 2.1 to 3.3 mm. Old-style low, narrow frets make string bending more difficult, but provide more accurate intonation.

Pickups | The two main types of pickups are single coil, as fitted to most Fenders, and humbuckers, as fitted to most Gibsons since 1957.

A single coil pickup as found on a Fender Strat consists of a coil of lacquered copper wire, which is wound around six 'slug' magnets – one for each string. As the guitar's strings vibrate they cut through the magnetic flux lines of the magnets, changing the magnetic field, and inducing a current in the pickup coils.

A humbucking pickup in essence consists of two single coil pickups placed side by side and wired in series. The two coils, however, are wired in opposite directions, one clockwise, one anti-clockwise, while the two sets of magnetic pole pieces feature opposite polarities. As far as a guitar string is concerned, these 'two' pickups are in phase – they add their signals to each other. As far as stray magnetic hum is concerned, however, the two pickups are out of phase – the signal generated in one coil cancels out the signal generated in the other.

There are several reasons for the difference in sound between humbucking and single coil pickups. Single coil pickups 'sense' the string at a single point; humbuckers 'sense' the string at two points some way apart, which makes them less sensitive to high harmonics. Humbuckers are louder, because they're sensing twice as much string, and generally feature more coil windings. Hence humbuckers have a fuller, richer sound, but generally lack the top end 'zing' of single coil pickups.

A pickup's basic tone is decided by the composition and shape of the magnets used, and the shape, gauge and number of turns of the pickup coils.

Most Gibson pickups, humbucking or non-humbucking, feature magnet(s) which sit below the coils, with adjustable pole pieces which focus the magnetic field towards the strings. Most Fender pickups up to the '70s feature slug style magnets which sit *inside* the coils – even their humbuckers, which were designed by Seth Lover, inventor of the PAF, after he left Gibson.

The number of windings and gauge of wire in the pickup coil also affects the sound; early Fender Strat pickups typically featured roughly 8,000 turns of 42AWG wire, which was reduced to 7,600 turns in the late '60s, giving more treble, but less output. A typical early Gibson PAF would feature 5,000 turns on each bobbin, making 10,000 in all. In either case, increasing the number of windings (and therefore coil impedance) increases output level, but at the expense of treble response. Increasing magnet strength increases output level; this can enable the use of fewer coil windings to give trebly, low impedance pickups.

Much research has been expended on designing humbucking pickups with the treble response of a humbucking pickup. These have centred on using two narrow coils, side by side (with 'blade' polepieces), or using two coils 'stacked' on top of each other. 'Active' pickups allow better impedance matching between guitar and amp; EMG pickups, for instance, employ a humbucking arrangement (which is 'stacked' on their Strat and Tele-style pickups) with a pre-amp encapsulated within the pickup casing, giving excellent rejection of interference.

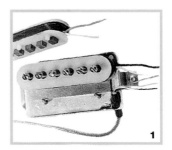
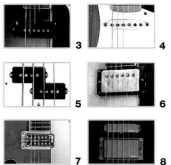

1. Humbucker magnet sits below coil
2. Single coil uses slug magnets within coil
3. Gibson P90 single coil pickup
4. Strat single coil pickup
5. Fender Precision bass split humbucker
6. Gibson PAF humbucker
7. Gretsch Filtertron humbucker features 12 adjustable polepieces and smaller magnets and coils than Gibson
8. EMG active pickups; 'single coil' pickup is in fact stacked humbucker

Pickup positioning is crucial to the sound produced by an electric guitar. Overtones vary along the string length, making optimum positioning a question of trial and error for designers. Using pickup combinations introduces a new element into the equation; a pair of pickups can often interact to give wonderful bell-like tones due to subtle phase cancellations; on seemingly identical guitars the same position can sound cheap and tinny. C'est la vie. The method of pickup mounting can also affect a guitar's sound; depending on whether it's mounted to the scratchplate, directly to the guitar's top, or – as in the Fender Telecaster – to the bridge plate.

Neck Joints | There are two main types of neck joint: glued-in or set necks, as used by Gibson and PRS, and bolt-on necks, as used by Fender and Music Man. A third type is the neck through body, as used in the Travis/Bigsby guitar, many Rickenbacker models, the Gibson Firebird, and the Jackson Soloist.

Regardless of tone, bolt-on necks are simpler and cheaper, and were introduced by Fender primarily for ease of repair and maintenance. Since then ease of production has become a major factor. Glued-in necks require higher constructional skills, while through-necks are notoriously expensive to produce; apart from anything else, they demand the use of a long length of quality timber – this is one of the reasons why many through-neck instruments use multi-laminates.

It may seem obvious, but the fit and stability of a neck joint is crucial on a guitar's tone. A tight bolted join can be just as efficient as a glued-in construction, but will still sound different due to the different ways in which vibrations are transmitted between body and neck. Thus many makers feel that a bolt-on neck gives more attack, while a glued-in neck gives a more compressed, sustained sound.

1. Bolt-on Strat joint
2. Set-in Les Paul neck joint
3. Set-in PRS joint
4. Jackson through-neck
5. Note Les Paul's set-back neck joint and headstock. It's more damage-prone than the Strat (6), but contributes to the guitar's sound

Headstock

A guitar's headstock is far more than just a place where you put the machineheads. According to many makers, including Tony Zemaitis, it has a substantial dampening effect which affects the guitar's sound.

There are two main types of headstock: the flat type, as used by Fender, and the tilt-back, as used by Gibson.

Fender used a flat headstock for several reasons. By reducing friction at the nut, tuning stability was improved; a straight string pull to the machineheads similarly reduced friction.

However, the back angle of a headstock has definite effect on a guitar's sound; Gibson moved from their initial 17° back angle to around 14° in the '70s; many believe the tone suffered as a result. According to Gibson's Tim Shaw: 'As you increase the headstock angle you increase string tension, which gives a firmer feel and a more pronounced attack.'

However, increasing headstock angle also increases friction at the nut; hence PRS guitars, for example, feature a reduced back angle on trem models compared to non-trem models.

Machine Heads

Early Gibson and Fender guitars used simple Kluson machine heads. By the '70s sealed designs by Grover and Schaller became fashionable; now locking machine heads are regarded as state of the art.

Locking machine heads in general limit the amount of string wrapped around the machine head post to around half a turn; this minimizes string stretching and speeds stringing-up. Tuning arrangements such as that of the Steinberger bass give a far more accurate tuning ratio – typically 40:1 – at the expense of the complete redesign of the instrument.

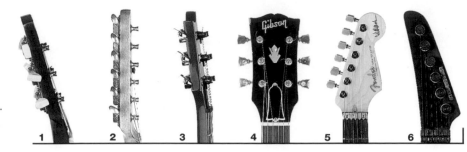

Nut

The guitar nut terminates the string and affects the tone of the open string.

The traditional nut material is bone; '50s Gretsches featured metal nuts for more sustain and subsequently zero frets which were intended to match the sound of open and fretted strings.

String hitching at the nut is a major cause of tuning problems with heavy tremolo usage. One solution is to lubricate the nut with, for example, graphite from a conventional pencil. Many modern nuts are made from 'slippery' graphite or teflon-based material to reduce this problem, while Trevor Wilkinson popularized 'roller' nuts for reduced friction.

1. Typical Gibson back-angled headstock (ES175)
2. Broadcaster/ Telecaster pioneered flat headstock
3. PRS has shallow back angle, locking heads and friction-reducing 'unobtanium' nut to reduce tuning problems
4. Three-a-side Gibson headstock is compact - but strings can hitch at nut
5. Jeff Beck Strat demonstrates 'straight string pull' of Fender design. This model features a Wilkinson roller nut
6. Steinberger uses locking machineheads and unique 'Knife Edge' nut, which uses six individual, movable elements to reduce friction

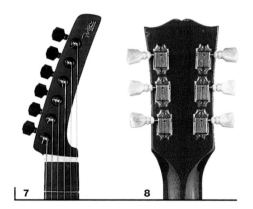

7. Parker Fly is modern version of Telecaster head, with straight string pull, low friction nut and locking machines
8. Les Paul Standard features simple Kluson machine heads. Compared with modern units, as these machine heads age they suffer from 'backlash;' the machine head may be turned some way before it affects the tuning

Bridge

A guitar bridge anchors the string and provides adjustment for height and intonation. There are three main types of non-trem bridges for solid body guitars: the wraparound bridge/tailpiece (Les Paul Jr or PRS Dragon), separate tune-o-matic bridge and stop bar tailpiece, as on the Les Paul Standard, and the Fender Tele or non-trem Strat style with through-body stringing. The choice between these designs is often dictated by the guitar's basic construction; a Gibson style bridge, for example, is much higher than that of a Strat or Tele, and requires a higher neck-to-body angle. The actual material used will also affect the guitar's sound; common material include mazak – an alloy commonly used in oriental guitars, brass, steel and aluminium, as used on Gibson wraparound bridge/tailpieces.

1: Gibson wraparound bridge/tailpiece
2: PRS Dragon uses similar principle, but is redesigned to reduce string breakage and improve intonation
3: Telecaster uses through-body stringing
4: Gibson tune-o-matic/stop bar combination

Tremolo Bridges

There are three common types of tremolo bridges: the Bigsby, the Strat type, and the Floyd Rose bridges (these should all, in fact, be referred to as vibrato units rather than tremolo units, but this misnomer has stuck).

The Bigsby tremolo is still used on modern Gretsch and Gibson guitars and allows for limited vibrato with minimum modification of the guitar, and a vintage appearance. However, return to pitch is erratic with heavy usage, even with the improved 'roller' bridges found on modern Gretsches.

The Stratocaster tremolo, a balanced fulcrum device which pivots on six screws, enables wider travel than the Bigsby, and provides better tuning stability by being part of a coherent whole, with, for example, straight string pull over the nut. It only allows minimal upbend, and still provides friction points which 'interpretations' such as those of PRS or Levinson seek to minimize.

The Floyd Rose is based on the Stratocaster balanced fulcrum principle, pivots on two screws, and avoids all friction points by clamping strings at the saddle and the nut. It dramatically improves tuning stability, to the extent that string stretching is the most significant problem. Many modern designs feature a Floyd Rose with a back rout, which enables significant upward bends. However, the Floyd Rose system is complex, expensive, and sounds different from a standard Strat trem.

1. Bigsby tremolo unit
2. Strat bridge/trem pivots on six screws
3. Floyd Rose features locking bridge saddles, and is used in combination with locking nut
4. Levinson Strat-derived design features roller saddles to reduce friction

Circuitry

Although many manufacturers have introduced complex systems, these have fallen out of fashion in favour of simple passive tone and volume controls. These consist of simple potentiometers; that of the volume control shunts an increasing amount of the voltage to ground, progressively reducing the output level, while the tone control shunts the output to ground via a capacitor; capacitors present less resistance to treble signals than to bass, thus treble is progressively reduced. Fender circuitry is notable for being mounted in modular fashion, attached to a scratchplate or control plate. Most Gibson systems are mounted into the wood of the guitar, requiring far more complex routing.

1. Gibson Les Paul controls
2. Tele wiring mounts on screening plate

Scale Length

Theoretical scale length is double the distance from the face of the nut to the centre of the 12th fret. The actual scale length is slightly greater – from the nut to the break point of the bridge saddle.

The two main scale lengths of the '50s were Gibson's nominal 24 3/4" and Fender's 25 1/2". Many modern guitars such as Music Man and PRS use a compromise 25" scale. Gibson's actual scale length has actually changed over the years, and is closer to 24.6" (624mm) than its nominal value.

Gibson's shorter scale length is easier on small hands, but the longer length of a Fender scale is often said to give a more defined, less muddy sound. Different scale lengths also give different string tension, which radically affects the feel – particularly when combined with the effect of the overall length of string from machine head to tailpiece.

Guitar Finish

The type of finish has always been acknowledged as having a major influence on the sound of an acoustic guitar. Its effect is now being acknowledged on the solid electric guitar, with thick finishes now being thought to inhibit a guitar's natural resonance.

Early Gibson and Fender guitars used thin, cellulose finishes. Many modern finishes are thicker and are usually polyester or polyurethane based. These look glossier, although at the moment there is a general move to a thinner, more traditional finish. Oiled finishes give a more natural feel, but need careful maintenance, otherwise the guitar's wood will absorb water, and become unstable.

1. Gretsch pioneered dramatic finishes, many of which were inherited from the company's drum range
2. Steve Vai pioneered a move to fluorescent finishes – and how!
3. Washburn Nuno Bettencourt N4 uses oiled finish for 'worn-in' feel

index

credits

The first edition of The Electric Guitar was produced to accompany the exhibition on The Electric Guitar at The Design Museum, Butlers Wharf, London (020 7-403 6933). The editor would like to thank the museum's Claire Catterall, Paul Thompson and John Hendry.
Jane Titterington, photo researcher for this edition, learned about obscure guitars in record time – thanks, Jane! Special thanks must go to Dave Burrluck and Tony Bacon for their invaluable help and advice. Guitars photographed came from the following individuals, and we are grateful for their help:
Doug Chandler of Chandler Guitars (020-8940 5874), Michael Cole, Bob Daisley, Barry Moorhouse at The Bass Centre (020-7265 1567), Alistair Morton, Ken Parker, Nick Rose, Dominic Salmon, Graeme Taylor, Chris Trigg, Helen Turner at John Hornby Skewes, Stuart Ward, Gary Winterflood, Rick Zsigmond at Fat Rick's Guitar Emporium (020-7370 7835)
Also thanks to the following for contributing help, information and interview material:
Paul Ashford, Tony Beasty, Jeff Beck, Christian Benker (Hofner), Ken Bran, James Burton, Richard Chapman, Mitch Colby (Korg US), Mike Cooper (Groove Tubes UK), Sylvia Corley, Jamie Crompton (Gibson London), Bill Cummiskey (Hoshino US), Larry DiMarzio, the sadly missed Willie Dixon, Bernard Docherty, Duane Eddy, Larry Fishman, Caesar Glebbeek (Hendrix Univibes magazine, tel/fax 353 2646 109), Rob Green (Status), Jeff Gould (Modulus Graphite), Buddy Guy, John Hall (Rickenbacker), Hank's Guitars, Tony Horkins, Cliff Jones, Steve Kaufman (IMC), BB King, Michael Leonard (The Guitar Magazine), Johnny Marr, Hank Marvin, J Mascis, John Mayall, Roger Mayer, Ted McCarty, Roger McGuinn, Charles Measures, Bill Nelson, Tom Nolan (Fender A&R Centre), Nigel Osborne, Les Paul, Marco Pirroni, JT Ribiloff (Gibson), Keith Richards, Paul Kurzeja, Linda Hancock and Elaine Cusack at Rock CD, Floyd Rose, Jane Rose, Tim Shaw (Gibson), Trevor Simpson, Neil Slaven, Dan Smith (Fender), Paul Reed Smith, Ned Steinberger, Rob Turner (EMG), Andrew Vaughan, Mike Vernon, Charlie Watkins, Natasha White, Richard Wooton, Steve Yelding (Marshall).

Bibliography
The following publications were used for research for this book:
Ken Achard *The History And Development Of The American Guitar* (Musical New Services 1977), Tony Bacon & Paul Day *The Ultimate Guitar Book (*Dorling Kindersley 1991), *The Fender Book* (Balafon 1992), *The Guru's Guitar Guide* (Track Record 1990), Julius Bellson *The Gibson Story* (Gibson 1973), Berry, Foose & Jones *Up From The Cradle Of Jazz* (University Of Georgia Press 1986), Chuck Berry *Chuck Berry: The Autobiography* (Harmony 1987), Ian Bishop *The Gibson Guitar From 1950* (Musical New Services 1977), *The Gibson Guitar From 1950 Vol 2* (Musical New Services 1979), Victor Bockris *Keith Richards: The Biography* (Hutchinson 1992), Patrick Carr (Ed): *The Illustrated History Of Country Music* (Dolphin 1980), Ray Coleman *Clapton* (Warner 1985), James Lincoln Collier *The Making Of Jazz* (MacMillan 1981), Cross, Flannigan & Preston *Led Zeppelin: Heaven and Hell* (Sidgwick & Jackson 1991), Helen Oakley Dance *Stormy Monday: The T-Bone Walker Story* (Da Capo 1987), Dellar, Thompson & Green *The Illustrated Encyclopedia of Country Music* (Salamander 1977), Ralph Denyer *The Guitar Handbook* (Dorling Kindersley 1982), Willie Dixon with Don Snowden *I Am The Blues* (Da Capo 1989), André Duchossoir *The Fender Telecaster* (Hal Leonard 1991), *The Fender Stratocaster* (Mediapresse 1988), *Gibson Electrics Vol 1* (Mediapresse 1981), *Guitar Identification* (Mediapresse 1983), Escott & Hawkins *Sun Records; The Brief History* (Quick Fox 1980) ,Tom & Mary Evans *Guitars: From The Renaissance To Rock* (OUP 1977), Charlie Gillett *The Sound Of The City* (Souvenir 1983), Ira Gitler *Jazz Masters Of The Forties* (Collier 1974), Glebbeek & Shapiro: *Jimi Hendrix: Electric Gypsy* (Mandarin 1992), John Hammond with Irving Townsend *Hammond On Record* (Penguin 1981), WC Handy *Father Of the Blues* (Collier 1970), Phil Hardy & Dave Laing *The Faber Companion to 20th Century Popular Music* (Faber & Faber 1990), Sheldon Harris *Blues Who's Who* (New Rochelle 1979), Allan Kozinn, Pete Welding, Dan Forte, Gene Santoro *The Guitar - The History, The Music, The Players* (Columbus 1984), Stephen LaVere: *Robert Johnson: The Complete Recordings* (sleeve notes, CBS, 1990), Mike Leadbitter & Neil Slaven *Blues Records 1943-66* (Oak 1968), Music Master:*The Official Musicmaster CD Catalogue* (Musicmaster 1992) Paul Oliver *The Story Of The Blues* (Penguin 1972), Robert Palmer *Deep Blues* (Penguin 1982), Gareth Pawlowski *How They Became The Beatles* (Macdonald 1990), Daffyd Rees & Luke Crampton *The Guinness Book Of Rock Stars* (Guinness 1990), Johnny Rogan *The Byrds* (Square One 1990), Charles Sawyer *BB King; The Authorised Biography* (Blandford 1981), Schnepel & Lemme *Electric Guitars Made In Germany* (Musik-Verlag Schnepel-Lemme 1987), Jay Scott *Gretsch – The Guitars Of The Fred Gretsch Company* (Centerstream 1992), Richard Smith *The Complete History of Rickenbacker Guitars* (Centerstream 1987), John Tobler (ed) *NME: The Rock'n'Roll Years* (Hamlyn 1992), Andrew Vaughan *The World Of Country Music* (Studio Editions 1992), Tom Wheeler *American Guitars* (Harper & Row 1982), *The Guitar Book* (Macdonald & Janes 1984).
Magazines used during research for this book include: *The Guitar Magazine* (UK), *Guitar Player* (US), *Guitar World* (US), *International Musician* (UK), *Guitarist* (UK), *Living Blues* (US), *Blues Unlimited* (UK), *Downbeat* (US) *Rolling Stone* (US)

discography

The following 100 selections will provide an aural accompaniment to this book's chapters on electric guitarists from 1935-2001. Bearing in mind that the electric guitar accounts for over half of the popular music of the last 50 years, this can only be a very brief introduction to the wealth of classic recordings available.

Various *Great Blues Guitarists: String Dazzlers* (CBS)
Definitive collection of early guitarists of the including Lonnie Johnson and Eddie Lang.

Various *The Slide Guitar: Bottles Knives and Steel* (CBS)
Superb remastered selection includes Charley Patton, Robert Johnson and Blind Willie Johnson.

Jimmie Lunceford *1934-1935* (Classics)
This big band material includes the first known amplified guitar on record, 'Hittin' The Bottle'.

Charlie Christian *The Genius Of the Electric Guitar* (CBS/Giants of Jazz)
Recordings by this superb guitarist seem to be issued then deleted with alarming regularity. Look out for anything he recorded with Benny Goodman, or his live Minton's recordings.

T-Bone Walker *Low Down Blues* (UK, Charly), *The Complete Recordings Of* (US, Mosaic)
Many Walker collections are patchy affairs - try and track down anything he recorded before 1954.

Django Reinhardt *Djangology* (RCA)
Admittedly, most of Reinhardt's classic material was on acoustic guitar, but no selection is complete without him.

Bob Wills and his Texas Playboys: *Anthology 1935-1973* (Rhino)

Guitar Slim *The Things I Used To Do* (Specialty/ Ace)

Chuck Berry *The Chess Box* (Chess/MCA)
Check out a greatest hits compilation if you must, but more comprehensive collections such as this box set prove Berry was far, far more than a one-riff wonder.

Chet Atkins *A Legendary Performer* (RCA)
A fair collection – also check out 1990's *Neck And Neck*, with Mark Knopfler.

Les Paul *The Legend and the Legacy* (Capitol)
This 4-CD box set shows off both Les Paul's guitaring skills and studio wizardry.

Muddy Waters *Best Of* (Chess/MCA)
Howlin' Wolf *Howlin' Wolf* (Chess/MCA)
Compilations from Chess' best-known bluesmen. Chess also produce box sets of each singer.

BB King *The Best Of BB King Volume One* (Ace/Flair), *Live At The Regal* (MCA)
20 excellent tracks from King's time on Kent records. King's MCA box set is good, but skips too briefly over his early work.

Elvis Presley *The King of Rock & Roll: The Complete '50s Masters* (RCA/BMG)
Excellent collection includes rare demos and alternative takes.

Various *The Sun Story* (Charly/ Rhino)
A stunning testimony to the talent-spotting and production talents of Sam Phillips.

Various *Chess Blues* (Chess/ MCA CHD4-9340)
Superlative 4-CD collection of Chess blues artists includes Howlin' Wolf, Muddy Waters, Lowell Fulson, Albert King, Otis Rush, Buddy Guy and more. Look out for The Chess rock'n'roll box set which includes vintage Chuck Berry, Bo Diddley, Dale Hawkins with James Burton, and more.

Freddie King *Taking Care Of Business* (Gusto/Charly)

Elmore James *Collection* (Deja Vu)

John Lee Hooker *The Ultimate Collection* (Rhino)

Jimmy Reed *The Best Of* (Crescendo)
From the musicianship of Freddie King to the superb nonmusicianship of Jimmy Reed, no guitar fan should be without records by these four bluesmen.

Eddie Cochran *C'Mon Everybody* (EMI)

Buddy Holly *20 Golden Greats* (MCA)
Two of the finest rock'n'roll guitarists to emerge from a country background.

Duane Eddy *Twangy Peaks* (EMI)

Link Wray *Walkin' With Link* (Epic)
Two '60s Eddy albums, on one CD, show Duane at his kitsch and twangy best. Link was his sinister alterego.

The Beatles *A Hard Day's Night, Rubber Soul, Revolver, The Beatles, Past Masters Volume 2* (EMI)
More than any other band, The Beatles defined the '60s. These albums in particular showed just how far a simple four piece band could go – both musically and culturally.

Bob Dylan *Live At The Albert Hall* (Sony), *Highway 61 Revisited* (CBS)
Dylan has made many sterling albums, but perhaps it's the one-time bootleg recording of his early electric concert at the Albert Hall that showed the collision of folk, blues and electricity at its then-controversial and still breathtaking best.

The Rolling Stones *The Rolling Stones, Beggars Banquet, Let It Bleed*, (London/Polygram) *Sticky Fingers, Exile On Main Street* (CBS)
From English R&B, inspired by Brian Jones, to their magnificent shambling height around 1970, these Stones albums are packed with classic songs.

The Yardbirds *Five Live Yardbirds* (Charly, UK), *Roger The Engineer* (Edsel, UK)
Five Live Yardbirds shows a young Eric Clapton already confident in the blues medium. *Roger The Engineer* is perhaps Jeff Beck's finest hour – the album's *Stroll On*, with Page, is proto-Zep.

John Mayall *Blues Breakers* (London)
A classic English blues album that demonstrates Mayall's genius as a band leader, and shows Clapton well on the way to God-like status.

The Kinks *The Collection* (Castle)

The Who *Who's Better Who's Best* (Polygram)
Two typically English bands who shared producer Shel Talmy; Dave Davies and Pete Townshend were at the vanguard of achieving heavier guitar sounds.

Jimi Hendrix *Are You Experienced, Axis Bold As Love, Electric Ladyland, The Ultimate Experience* (Polydor)

Best remembered for his high volume, high octane axe heroics, these albums reveal Hendrix as sensitive singer/ songwriter, soulman, and much more.

Cream *Wheels Of Fire, Strange Brew* (Polydor)
Much of this prototype supergroup's material was patchy, but studio album *Wheels of Fire* and the *Strange Brew* compilation show Clapton, Bruce and Baker at their best.

Fleetwood Mac *Greatest Hits* (Sony)
Songs like 'Oh Well' and 'Man Of The World' show that Peter Green's songwriting skills were as impressive as his guitar-playing abilities; both were tragically short-lived.

Free *Fire And Water* (A&M)
Premier British blues-rock

Albert King *The Best Of Albert King* (Stax/Ace)
This blues player's finest moment came when he joined the Stax label in 1966, as his deleted first album, *Born Under A Bad Sign*, and this compilation demonstrate.

The Byrds *Mr Tambourine Man, Sweetheart Of The Rodeo* (Columbia)
Partly inspired by The Beatles, The Byrds went on to explore distinctly western influences on *Sweetheart*, with stringbending champion Clarence White.

The Beach Boys *Pet Sounds, Smiley Smile/Wild Honey* (Capitol)

The Doors *The Doors* (Elektra)

The Grateful Dead *Workingman's Dead* (WEA)
Despite the focus on England, there was no shortage of great American guitar-based music in the '60s, as these bands, among many others, illustrate.

Quicksilver Messenger Service *Happy Trails* (BGO)
Guitarist John Cippolina was a pioneer of the freeform West Coast guitar sound

Various *Nuggets* (Rhino)

Various *Pebbles Vols 1&2* (AIP)

The Velvet Underground *The Velvet Underground & Nico, White Light White Heat, The Velvet Underground, VU* (Polydor)

MC5 *Kick Out The Jams* (Elektra)

Blue Cheer *Louder Than God; The Best Of* (Rhino)

The Stooges *The Stooges* (Elektra)
Something wonderfully sick was stirring in the USA. From the lamebrained punks of *Nuggets* and *Pebbles*, through the intellectual thuggery of the Velvet Underground, to the early metal of MC5 and Blue Cheer, most of these bands were commercial failures – but later became legends.

Led Zeppelin *Led Zeppelin 1, 2, Four Symbols* (Atlantic)
Often imitated, Zep combined Jimmy Page's guitar bombast with songwriting and production skills that eluded most of their successors.

James Brown *Star Time* (Polydor)

Booker T & the MGs *Best Of* (Atlantic)

Funkadelic *Maggot Brain* (Westbound/Ace)
The electric guitar also ruled the roost in '60s soul. James Brown's stripped-down backings were some of the most instrumentally-impressive guitar outings of the decade; MG Steve Cropper similarly

employed an exemplary, economical approach. Then that all changed as Funkadelic adopted all the excess of their rock cousins, heavily influencing Prince.

Santana *Santana, Abraxas* (CBS)
Combining psychedelic blues and latin rhythms, Carlos Santana's first albums, before his band was beset by constant personnel changes, remain his best.

Neil Young *After the Goldrush, Harvest, Decades* (Reprise)
Young might not play lots of notes but he's one of the world's finest guitarists – echoes can be heard, for instance, in the sound of Dinosaur Jr.

Black Sabbath *Paranoid* (WEA)

Deep Purple *Machinehead* (WEA)
Pioneering, gloriously ludicrous metal which provided countless memorable riffs, coming soon to your ringtone!

Mahavishnu Orchestra *Birds Of Fire* (Columbia)

Jeff Beck *Blow By Blow* (Epic)
Before it disappeared up its own improvised backside, fusion looked like the way ahead for rock music. These two albums remain the finest of the genre.

Pink Floyd *Piper At The Gates Of Dawn, Dark Side Of The Moon* (EMI)
When Syd Barrett turned from whimsy to lunacy, Dave Gilmour and bassist Roger Waters took over. *Dark Side...* has hardly been out of the charts since its release.

Roy Buchanan *That's What I'm Here For* (Polydor)
Who knows if he really turned down a job in the Stones, but Buchanan was definitely one of the Tele's finest exponents.

Steely Dan *Pretzel Logic* (MCA)

The Eagles *Hotel California* (Asylum)
Both obscenely melodic and tasteful, Steely Dan and The Eagles helped define the FM rock genre, and boasted consummate guitarists in the shape of Skunk Baxter and Joe Walsh.

The Ramones *The Ramones* (Sire)

Patti Smith *Horses* (Arista)

Television *Marquee Moon* (Elektra)

The Sex Pistols *Never Mind the Bollocks* (Virgin)
Four manifestos for the punk movement.

Van Halen *Van Halen 1* (WEA)
Eddie Van Halen reinvents rock guitar. The track *Eruption*, in particular, has acquired exalted status.

Talking Heads *More Songs About Buildings and Food* (Sire)
Intelligent postpunk powered by the off beat edge of David Byrne and exemplary bassplaying of Tina Weymouth.

Dire Straits *Dire Straits* (Vertigo)
Less media-hungry than the punks, Mark Knopfler's crew would out-sell them all.

Nirvana *Nevermind* (Geffen)
The 'alternative' sound of Pixies and Slint hits the mainstream, thrillingly revitalises pop music – and kills off 'hair' bands.

Rage Against The Machine *Rage Against The Machine* (Epic)

Radiohead *OK Computer* (Parlophone)
Tom Morello and Jonny Greenwood demonstrate the virtuoso lead guitarist is still relevant in the electronic era.

White Stripes *De Stijl* (Sympathy For The Record Industry)
A loud guitar and drums. Which is more or less where we came in.